The Threat Intelligence Handbook

A Practical Guide for Security Teams to Unlocking the Power of Intelligence

Edited by Chris Pace
Foreword by Dr. Christopher Ahlberg

CYBEREDGE
P R E S S

The Threat Intelligence Handbook

Published by:
CyberEdge Group, LLC
1997 Annapolis Exchange Parkway
Suite 300
Annapolis, MD 21401
(800) 327-8711
www.cyber-edge.com

For general information on CyberEdge Group research and marketing consulting services, or to create a custom *Definitive Guide* book for your organization, contact our sales department at 800-327-8711 or info@cyber-edge.com.

ISBN: 978-0-9990354-6-7 (paperback)
ISBN: 978-0-9990354-7-4 (eBook)

Printed in the United States of America.

10 9 8 7 6 5 4 3 2 1

Publisher's Acknowledgements

CyberEdge Group thanks the following individuals for their respective contributions:

Editor: Susan Shuttleworth
Graphic Design: Debbi Stocco
Production Coordinator: Jon Friedman

Contributors

Chris Pace (editor and contributor) works for Recorded Future to engage and educate audiences on the power of intelligence-driven security. Before beginning a career in security, Chris trained as a broadcast journalist and also has worked in IT departments in the public and private sectors.

Andrei Barysevich (contributor) specializes in the analysis of intelligence from cybercriminal communities at Recorded Future. Andrei has worked as an independent e-commerce fraud researcher, and a private consultant for the FBI's cybercrime unit.

Levi Gundert (contributor) has spent the past 20 years in both the government and the private sector, defending networks, arresting international criminals, and uncovering nation-state adversaries. He has held senior information security leadership positions across technology and financial services startups and enterprises. He is a trusted risk advisor to Fortune 500 companies, and a prolific speaker, blogger, and columnist.

Allan Liska (contributor) is a senior security architect at Recorded Future. Allan has more than 15 years of experience in information security, authoring numerous books and working as both a security practitioner and an ethical hacker.

Maggie McDaniel (contributor) is senior director of Recorded Future's Insikt Group research team. With more than 15 years of experience in threat intelligence tradecraft, analysis, and production, Maggie's previous roles include director of intelligence production at Fidelity Investments.

John Wetzel (contributor) heads up training at Recorded Future. John's previous role was as a counterintelligence special agent with the Department of Defense, where he worked with the U.S. defense community to defend against foreign threats targeting the nation's technologies.

Foreword by **Dr. Christopher Ahlberg**, co-founder and CEO, Recorded Future.

Table of Contents

Foreword

When you hear the word "intelligence," you may think of MI6, the CIA, the KGB, or perhaps even SPECTRE (the SPecial Executive for Counterintelligence, Terrorism, Revenge, and Extortion).

And it is true that threat intelligence in the information technology world includes elements of James Bond stories: criminal masterminds and nation-state actors scheming to steal vast sums and sow confusion in the civilized world, insidious cyber weapons capable of wreaking havoc on the unwary, and dark corners where shady evildoers gather to recruit accomplices and plot their next crime.

Fortunately for those of us on the ground managing the day-to-day grind of threat intelligence, this is about as far as we can take this analogy. Modern threat intelligence is not just the province of a few elite secret agents. On the contrary, the application of intelligence is a team sport with measurable impact on day-to-day operations.

While there are expert analysts who understand the tools, techniques, and procedures of sophisticated threat actors and can gain access to restricted forums on the dark web, the work they do is only made actionable when put into the hands of those at the front line of network defense. Members of the SOC team, the incident response team, the vulnerability management team, and others can use the intelligence they uncover to find and block ongoing attacks and prevent recurrences. And security leaders can get insight into emerging trends and increased risk.

Intelligence can spearhead a highly proactive security strategy when it can be consumed by the teams and technology able to make the best use of it.

This book will explain how you can begin the process of democratizing threat intelligence and put it into the hands of the people in your organization who can use it effectively. We look at the specific threat intelligence needs of six security teams, the sources of that intelligence, and exactly how the teams can use it to improve their decision making. We also look at frameworks that can help each team organize and prioritize its activities and provide advice on how to start up and grow your organization's threat intelligence program.

The subtitle of this book starts with "A Practical Guide ..." and our intention is to live up to the adjective "practical." We are offering information and advice that you can apply today to solve real-world problems with threat intelligence.

I want to thank everyone at Recorded Future, our users and customers, and the industry experts who have contributed to the contents of this book. As you can see from the "Contributors" list in the front, we have compiled knowledge from many of our most experienced and innovative people.

We hope you will find this book an informative companion as you apply threat intelligence to address the security challenges you face.

Dr. Christopher Ahlberg
Co-Founder and CEO
Recorded Future

Introduction

I t's easy to find descriptions of what threat intelligence is. But it's harder to learn how to use it to truly make your organization safe from cybercriminals. How can threat intelligence strengthen all the teams in a cybersecurity organization?

This book answers this question. It reviews the kinds of threat intelligence that are useful to security teams and how each team can use that intelligence to solve problems and address challenges. It discusses how security analysts in the real world use threat intelligence to decide what alerts to investigate (or ignore), what incidents to escalate, and what vulnerabilities to patch. It examines how information collected outside of the enterprise can help model risks more accurately and prevent fraud.

We invite you to learn about how threat intelligence can help everyone in cybersecurity anticipate problems, respond faster to attacks, and make better decisions on how to reduce risk.

Chapters at a Glance

Chapter 1, "Intelligence-Driven Security," describes the phases of the threat intelligence lifecycle and looks at sources of threat intelligence.

Chapter 2, "Threat Intelligence for Security Operations," explores how intelligence provides context for triage and helps the SOC team make better decisions.

Chapter 3, "Threat Intelligence for Incident Response," discusses how intelligence can minimize reactivity in incident response and presents three use cases.

Chapter 4, "Threat Intelligence for Vulnerability Management," examines how intelligence helps prioritize vulnerabilities based on true risk to the enterprise.

Chapter 5, "Threat Intelligence for Security Leaders," explores how building a comprehensive threat intelligence capability can help CISOs manage risk and make effective investment decisions.

Chapter 6, "Threat Intelligence for Risk Analysis," explains the value of risk models and how intelligence can provide hard data about attack probabilities and costs.

Chapter 7, "Threat Intelligence for Fraud Prevention," enumerates how intelligence can help anticipate and defeat fraud.

Chapter 8, "Analytical Frameworks for Threat Intelligence," explains how three leading threat frameworks provide structures for thinking about attacks.

Chapter 9, "Your Threat Intelligence Journey," provides suggestions on how to start simple and scale up a threat intelligence program.

Chapter 10, "Developing the Core Threat Intelligence Team," describes how a dedicated team can take threat intelligence to a new level.

Helpful Icons

 TIP Tips provide practical advice that you can apply in your own organization.

 DON'T FORGET When you see this icon, take note, as the related content contains key information that you won't want to forget.

 CAUTION Proceed with caution because if you don't, it may prove costly to you and your organization.

 TECH TALK Content associated with this icon is more technical in nature and is intended for IT practitioners.

 ON THE WEB Want to learn more? Follow the corresponding URL to discover additional content available on the web.

Chapter 1

Intelligence-Driven Security

- Examine the phases of the threat intelligence lifecycle
- Review sources of threat intelligence
- Look at the roles of threat intelligence tools and human analysts

"Every battle is won before it is ever fought."

— Sun Tzu

What Have You Heard About Threat Intelligence?

You may have heard threat intelligence discussed at a conference or trade show. Perhaps you were informed by a consultant that threat intelligence can reduce the time you spend investigating security events. Maybe you read a report about state-sponsored attacks and want to know how to protect your enterprise. You have probably noticed that in organizations from multinational enterprises to midmarket companies, information security teams are racing to add threat intelligence to their security program.

But you may also have heard some misconceptions: that threat intelligence is just data feeds and PDF reports, or is simply a research service for the incident response team, or requires a dedicated team of high-priced, elite analysts.

These are fallacies! In this book we will show that threat intelligence:

☑ Includes information and analysis from a rich array of sources, presented in ways that make it easy to understand and use

☑ Is immensely valuable to all the major teams in the cybersecurity organization

☑ Can be handled mostly by the existing security staff (with the right tools and support)

In fact, threat intelligence solves many problems for cybersecurity organizations. For example, security operations teams are challenged by an overwhelming volume of alerts; threat intelligence adds valuable context around indicators of compromise (IOCs) and helps triage security incidents. Incident responders struggle to fully contain and remediate intrusions; intelligence provides real-time information to contain, hunt, and eradicate threats. Senior leaders have critical questions on the impact of immediate security events and the cost of future events; intelligence helps answer many of those concerns.

To see why threat intelligence can be so useful to so many, let's review its lifecycle.

The Six Phases of the Threat Intelligence Lifecycle

Threat intelligence is built on analytic techniques honed over several decades by government and military agencies. Traditional intelligence focuses on six distinct phases that make up what is called the "intelligence cycle":

1. Direction
2. Collection
3. Processing
4. Analysis
5. Dissemination
6. Feedback

Figure 1-1 shows how those six phases align with threat intelligence.

Figure 1-1: Threat intelligence and the six phases of the intelligence lifecycle.

Direction

The direction phase of the lifecycle is when you set goals for the threat intelligence program. This involves understanding and articulating:

☑ The information assets and business processes that need to be protected

☑ The potential impacts of losing those assets or interrupting those processes

☑ The types of threat intelligence that the security organization requires to protect assets and respond to threats

☑ Priorities about what to protect

Once high-level intelligence needs are determined, an organization can formulate questions that channel the need for information into discrete requirements. For example, if a goal is to understand likely adversaries, one logical question would be, "Which actors on underground forums are actively soliciting data concerning our organization?"

A Library of Goals

Recorded Future has created a list of pre-configured intelligence goals that includes the most common intelligence requirements of Global 500 organizations. This list helps companies starting out with threat intelligence think about their issues and priorities and decide how threat intelligence can be plugged into their existing processes. Selected goals from this library are included in the appendix of this book.

Adversarial models such as the Lockheed Martin Cyber Kill Chain and the MITRE Adversarial Tactics, Techniques & Common Knowledge (ATT&CK) matrix (discussed in Chapter 8), can also help companies focus on the types of threat intelligence they need to collect to prevent breaches.

Collection

Collection is the process of gathering information to address the most important intelligence requirements. Information gathering can occur organically through a variety of means, including:

- ☑ Pulling metadata and logs from internal networks and security devices
- ☑ Subscribing to threat data feeds from industry organizations and cybersecurity vendors
- ☑ Holding conversations and targeted interviews with knowledgeable sources
- ☑ Scanning open source news and blogs
- ☑ Scraping and harvesting websites and forums
- ☑ Infiltrating closed sources such as dark web forums

The data collected typically will be a combination of finished information, such as intelligence reports from cybersecurity experts and vendors, and raw data, like malware signatures or leaked credentials on a paste site.

Threat Intelligence Sources

Technical sources (e.g., threat feeds) — Available in huge quantities, often for free. Technical sources are easy to integrate with existing security technologies but often contain a high proportion of false positives and outdated results.

Media (e.g., security websites, vendor research) — These sources often provide useful information about emerging threats but are hard to connect with technical indicators in order to measure risk.

Social media — Social channels offer huge amounts of valuable data, but it comes at a price. False positives and misinformation are rampant, so determining which insights are usable requires a tremendous amount of cross-referencing with other sources.

Threat actor forums — Specifically designed to host relevant discussions, forums offer some of the most helpful insights available anywhere. Once again, though, analysis and cross-referencing are essential to determine what is truly valuable.

The dark web (including markets and forums) — While often the birthplace of hugely valuable intelligence, dark web sources can be extremely hard to access, particularly those that play host to serious criminal communities.

DON'T FORGET You need multiple sources of intelligence to get a complete picture of potential and actual threats. As shown in Figure 1-1, they include **internal sources** like firewall and router logs, network packet capture tools, and vulnerability scans, **technical sources** such as vulnerability databases and threat data feeds, and **human sources**, including traditional and social media, cybersecurity forums and blogs, and dark web forums. Missing any one of these can slow down investigations and cause gaps in remediation.

TIP Automate! Analysts should spend as little time as possible collecting data, and as much time as possible evaluating and communicating threat information.

ON THE WEB Confused about the difference between threat intelligence sources, feeds, platforms, and providers? Read the Recorded Future blog post "Threat Intelligence: Difference Between Platforms and Providers."

Processing

Processing is the transformation of collected information into a format usable by the organization. Almost all raw data collected needs to be processed in some manner, whether by humans or machines.

Different collection methods often require different means of processing. Human reports may need to be correlated and ranked, deconflicted, and checked. An example might be extracting IP addresses from a security vendor's report and adding them to a CSV file for importing to a security information and event management (SIEM) product. In a more technical area, processing might involve extracting indicators from an email, enriching them with other information, and then communicating with endpoint protection tools for automated blocking.

TIP

Automate more! With the right tools, most processing workflows, as well as most collection processes, can be automated. For example, a security automation tool might identify a suspicious IOC, then conduct a sequence of checks to bring context to the IOC. This saves the analyst from having to conduct those checks manually.

Analysis

Analysis is a human process that turns processed information into intelligence that can inform decisions. Depending on the circumstances, the decisions might involve whether to investigate a potential threat, what actions to take immediately to block an attack, how to strengthen security controls, or how much investment in additional security resources is justified.

DON'T FORGET

Analysts must have a clear understanding of who is going to be using their intelligence and what decisions those people make. You want the intelligence you deliver to be perceived as actionable, not as academic. Most of this book is devoted to giving you a clear picture of exactly how threat intelligence can improve decision making and actions in different areas of cybersecurity.

The form in which the information is presented is especially important. It is useless and wasteful to collect and process information and then deliver it in a form that can't be understood and used by the decision maker.

For example, if you want to communicate with non-technical leaders, your report must:

- ☑ Be concise (a one-page memo or a handful of slides)
- ☑ Avoid confusing and overly technical terms and jargon
- ☑ Articulate the issues in business terms (such as direct and indirect costs and impact on reputation)
- ☑ Include a recommended course of action

Some intelligence may need to be delivered in a variety of formats for different audiences, say, by a live video feed and a PowerPoint presentation. Not all intelligence needs to be digested via a formal report. Successful threat intelligence teams provide continual technical reporting to other security teams with external context around IOCs, malware, threat actors, vulnerabilities, and threat trends.

Dissemination

Dissemination involves getting the finished intelligence output to the places it needs to go.

As illustrated in Figure 1-1, most cybersecurity organizations have at least six teams that can benefit from threat intelligence. For each of these audiences you need to ask:

- ☑ What threat intelligence do they need, and how can external information support their activities?
- ☑ How should the intelligence be presented to make it easily understandable and actionable for that audience?
- ☑ How often should we provide updates and other information?
- ☑ Through what media should the intelligence be disseminated?
- ☑ How should we follow up if they have questions?

Feedback

As you have no doubt gathered, we believe that it is critically important to understand your overall intelligence priorities and the requirements of the security teams that will be consuming the threat intelligence. Their needs guide all phases of the intelligence lifecycle and tell you:

☑ What types of data to collect

☑ How to process and enrich the data to turn it into useful information

☑ How to analyze the information and present it as actionable intelligence

☑ To whom each type of intelligence must be disseminated, how quickly it needs to be disseminated, and how fast to respond to questions

You need regular feedback to make sure you understand the requirements of each group, and to make adjustments as their requirements and priorities change.

For every "customer" team, establish both a channel for fast, informal feedback (such as an email address, an internal forum, or a team collaboration tool) and a formal, structured surveying process (such as an online survey or a quarterly face-to-face meeting). The informal channel helps you react and adjust immediately, while the structured survey ensures that you get input from everyone and can track your progress over time.

Tools and People

Tools are essential to automating the collection, processing, and dissemination steps in the intelligence lifecycle and to supporting and accelerating analysis. Without the right tools, analysts will spend all their time on the mechanical aspects of these tasks and never have time for real analysis.

Most mature threat intelligence groups leverage two types of tools:

- ☑ Threat intelligence solutions that are designed to collect, process, and analyze all types of threat data from internal, technical, and human sources
- ☑ Existing security tools, such as SIEMs and security analytics tools, which collect and correlate security events and log data

Human analysts are equally if not more important. You can't rely on tools to interview security experts and probe closed dark web forums, and you need people to analyze and synthesize intelligence for the people in the security organization and management who will consume it.

The analysts do not need to belong to a central, elite threat intelligence department. While someone needs to take an organization-wide view of the threat intelligence function, make decisions about resources and priorities, and track progress, we have seen many successful organizational structures. You could have a central group with dedicated threat intelligence analysts, or a small group inside the incident response (IR) or security operations center (SOC) organizations. Alternatively, members of the different cybersecurity groups can be responsible for analyzing threat intelligence for their colleagues.

In Chapter 9 we discuss how the organizational structure often evolves as the threat intelligence function matures. In Chapter 10 we provide advice on how to organize a core threat intelligence team.

Chapter 2

Threat Intelligence for Security Operations

- See how "alert fatigue" risks undoing the good work of security operations centers (SOCs)
- Understand the value of context for improving triage
- Learn how threat intelligence can lead to less wasted time and better decisions by the SOC team

"Being the worst makes you first."

— Sign in hospital emergency room

Most security operations center (SOC) teams find themselves hostages to the huge volumes of alerts generated by the networks they monitor. Triaging these alerts takes too long, and many are never investigated at all. "Alert fatigue" leads analysts to take alerts less seriously than they should.

Threat intelligence provides an antidote to many of these problems. Among other uses, it can be employed to filter out false alarms, speed up triage, and simplify incident analysis.

Responsibilities of the SOC Team

On paper, the responsibilities of the SOC team seem simple:

- ☑ **Monitor** for potential threats
- ☑ **Detect** suspicious network activity
- ☑ **Contain** active threats
- ☑ **Remediate** using available technology

When a suspicious event is detected, the SOC team investigates, then works with other security teams to reduce the impact and severity of the attack. You can think of the roles and responsibilities within a SOC as being similar to those of emergency services teams responding to 911 calls, as shown in Figure 2-1.

Stage	Role	Responsibilities
Triage	Operator (911 Center) Security Analyst (SOC)	Determine the relevance and urgency of each incoming alert. Decide if the alert is legitimate and should be escalated.
First Response	First Responder (911) Incident Responder (SOC)	Determine the scope of the incident. Identify affected and vulnerable systems. Recommend actions to contain the effects.
Investigation	Detective (911) Threat Hunter (SOC)	Determine root causes and weaknesses in defenses. Recommend actions to prevent recurrences.

Figure 2-1: The roles and responsibilities of emergency services teams and SOC teams are similar.

The Overwhelming Volume of Alerts

Over the past several years, most enterprises have added new types of threat detection technologies to their networks. Every tool sounds the alarm when it sees anomalous or suspicious behavior. In combination, these tools can create a cacophony of security alerts. Security analysts are simply unable to review, prioritize, and investigate all these alerts on their own. Because of alert fatigue, all too often they ignore alerts, chase false positives, and make mistakes.

Research confirms the magnitude of these problems. Industry analyst firm ESG asked cybersecurity professionals about their biggest security operations challenge, and 35 percent said it was "keeping up with the volume of security alerts." In its 2018 State of the SOC report, SIEM provider Exabeam revealed that SOCs are understaffed according to 45 percent of professionals who work in them, and of those, 63 percent think they could use anywhere from two to 10 additional employees. Cisco's 2018 Security Capabilities Benchmark study found that organizations can investigate only 56 percent of the security alerts they receive on a given day, and of those investigated alerts, only 34 percent are deemed legitimate (Figure 2-2).

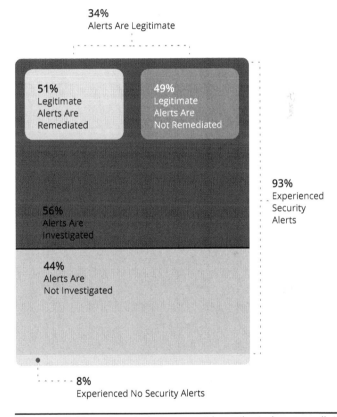

34%
Alerts Are Legitimate

51%
Legitimate
Alerts Are
Remediated

49%
Legitimate
Alerts Are
Not Remediated

93%
Experienced
Security
Alerts

56%
Alerts Are
Investigated

44%
Alerts Are
Not Investigated

8%
Experienced No Security Alerts

Figure 2-2: Many threat alerts are not investigated or remediated. (Source: Cisco)

Context Is King

At its heart, threat intelligence for the SOC is about enriching internal alerts with the external information and context necessary to make risk-based decisions. Context is critical for rapid triage, and also very important for scoping and containing incidents.

Triage requires lots of context

A huge part of an average SOC analyst's day is spent responding to alerts generated by internal security systems, such as SIEM or EDR technologies. Sources of internal data are vital in identifying potentially malicious network activity or a data breach.

Unfortunately, this data is often difficult to interpret in isolation. Determining if an alert is relevant and urgent requires gathering related information (context) from a wide variety of internal system logs, network devices, and security tools (Figure 2-3), *and* from external threat databases. Searching all of these threat data sources for context around each alert is hugely time consuming.

Key Aspects		Security Monitoring Requirement
	Business Traffic Crossing a Boundary	Traffic exchanges are authorized and conform to security policy. Transport of malicious content and other forms of attack by manipulation of business traffic are detected and alerted.
	Activity at a Boundary	Detect suspect activity indicative of the actions of an attacker attempting to breach the system boundary or other deviation from normal business behavior.
	Internal Workstation, Server, or Device	Detect changes to device status and configuration from accidental or deliberate acts by a user or by malware.
	Internal Network Activity	Detect suspicious activity that may indicate attacks by internal users or external attackers who have penetrated the internal network.
	Network Connections	Prevent unauthorized connections to the network made by remote access, VPN, wireless, or any other transient means of network connection.
	Session Activity By User and Workstation	Detect unauthorized activity and access that is suspicious or violates security policy requirements.
	Alerting on Events	Be able to respond to security incidents in a time frame appropriate to the perceived criticality of the incident.
	Accurate Time in Logs	Be able to correlate event data collected from disparate sources.
	Data Backup Status	Be able to recover from an event that compromises the integrity or availability of information assets.

Figure 2-3: Key aspects of security monitoring and internal sources of context. (Source: UK NCSC)

Use case: Correlating and enriching alerts

An analyst attempting to triage an initial alert without access to enough context is like a person trying to understand a news story after reading just the headline. Even when the analyst has access to external information in the form of threat feeds (Figure 2-4), that information is very hard to assimilate and correlate with other data related to the alert.

2018-09-13 02:46:26	E	63.153.27.53	offline
2018-09-12 21:41:44	E	75.130.100.165	online
2018-09-12 18:54:45	E	71.172.252.50	online
2018-09-12 15:51:16	E	118.189.9.243	offline
2018-09-12 14:11:41	E	31.167.248.50	offline
2018-09-12 08:32:01	E	78.134.74.39	online
2018-09-12 05:03:02	E	42.114.73.81	offline
2018-09-12 04:56:53	E	216.59.200.206	offline
2018-09-11 11:35:10	E	183.82.97.20	offline
2018-09-11 08:59:59	E	128.2.98.139	offline
2018-09-11 08:12:12	E	47.38.231.174	offline
2018-09-11 08:01:28	E	217.36.122.251	offline
2018-09-11 07:45:59	E	107.184.160.132	offline
2018-09-11 06:45:54	E	71.75.206.192	online
2018-09-11 06:43:49	E	123.231.21.141	offline
2018-09-11 05:54:51	E	189.222.75.8	offline
2018-09-11 05:54:51	E	189.211.177.113	offline
2018-09-11 05:54:51	E	92.27.115.15	offline
2018-09-11 05:54:51	E	207.107.101.210	offline

Figure 2-4: It is very difficult to find relevant information in a raw threat feed and correlate it with other data related to an alert.

Threat intelligence, or more precisely, information delivered through a threat intelligence solution, can completely transform the situation. Such a solution has the capability to automatically enrich threat data into intelligence and correlate it with alerts, as illustrated in Figure 2-5. The context provided might include first and most recent references to a piece of malware or a suspicious IP address, the number of sightings, associations with attack types and specific threat actors, and descriptions of the behavior of the malware or the uses of the IP address (say, as part of a botnet).

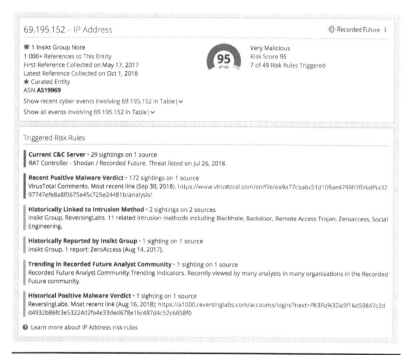

Figure 2-5: A threat intelligence solution can automatically enrich alerts with context such as previous sightings, associations with attack types and threat actors, and risk scores. (Source: Recorded Future)

This enrichment enables SOC analysts to quickly identify the most significant threats and take immediate, informed actions to resolve them.

Enrichment allows relatively junior analysts in the SOC to "punch above their weight" by making connections that otherwise would have required more experience. It also provides a form of accelerated on-the-job training by providing in-depth information about the latest threats.

TECH TALK As an example of upskilling relatively junior analysts, suppose an alert is generated when an unknown external IP address attempts to connect over TCP port 445. Experienced analysts might know that a recent exploit for SMB has been used by ransomware to propagate itself and would identify the IP as likely compromised based on the owner, location, and open source data. Newer analysts might not be able to make these connections unaided, but contextualized threat intelligence could show them that other devices on the network use SMB on port 445 to transfer files and data between servers. It could also inform them that the new exploit and ransomware have been associated with that IP address.

Improving the "Time to No"

As important as it is for SOC analysts to gather information about real threats more quickly and accurately, there is an argument to be made that *the ability to rapidly rule out false alarms is even more important.*

Threat intelligence provides SOC staff with additional information and context needed to triage alerts promptly and with far less effort. It can prevent analysts from wasting hours pursuing alerts based on:

☑ Actions that are more likely to be innocuous rather than malicious

☑ Attacks that are not relevant to that enterprise

☑ Attacks for which defenses and controls are already in place

Some threat intelligence solutions automatically perform much of this filtering by customizing risk feeds to ignore or downgrade alerts that do not match organization- and industry-specific criteria.

Threat Intelligence Makes IT Security Teams 32 Percent More Efficient

A survey and analysis by IDC found that a threat intelligence solution enabled IT security teams to reduce the time needed for threat investigation, threat resolution, and security report compilation by **32 percent**, saving an average of **$640,000 annually**. In addition, the teams in the survey were able to detect **22 percent** more threats before they impacted the organization, and resolve incidents **63 percent** faster. To read the full IDC white paper, go to https://go.recordedfuture.com/idc.

Beyond Triage

As well as accelerating triage, threat intelligence can help SOC teams simplify incident analysis and containment.

For example, by revealing that a certain piece of malware is often used by cybercriminals as the first step in an attack on financial applications, the SOC team can start monitoring those applications more closely and home in on other evidence of that attack type.

Chapter 3

Threat Intelligence for Incident Response

In this chapter

- Learn how threat intelligence can minimize reactivity
- Review characteristics of threat intelligence solutions that make them effective for meeting incident response challenges
- Explore use cases for using threat intelligence for incident response

"Care shouldn't start in the emergency room."

— James Douglas

O f all security groups, incident response teams are perhaps the most highly stressed. Among the reasons:

☑ Cyber incident volumes have increased steadily for two decades.

☑ Threats have become more complex and harder to analyze; staying on top of the shifting threat landscape has become a major task in itself.

☑ When responding to security incidents, analysts are forced to spend a lot of time manually checking and disseminating data from disparate sources.

☑ Containment of attacks and eradication of vulnerabilities continually grows more difficult.

As a result, incident response teams routinely operate under enormous time pressures and often are unable to contain cyber incidents promptly.

Continuing Challenges

While it's difficult to be precise about the number of incidents experienced by a typical organization, there is no doubt that cyberattack volume is growing rapidly. According to SonicWall, the global volume of malware attacks increased by more than 18 percent during 2017 alone. Other popular attack vectors, such as encrypted traffic and phishing, are also seeing substantial increases in volume every year. While some of this growing pressure is mitigated by preventative technologies, a huge additional strain is nonetheless being placed on incident response teams because of the following factors.

A skills gap

Incident response is not an entry-level security function. It encompasses a vast swath of skills, including static and dynamic malware analysis, reverse engineering, digital forensics, and more. It requires analysts who have experience in the industry and can be relied upon to perform complex operations under pressure.

The highly publicized cybersecurity skills gap has grown consistently wider over the past decade. According to a 2017 research report by ISSA, almost three-quarters of security professionals claim their organization is affected by the global skills shortage. In their most recent Global Information Security Workforce Study, Frost & Sullivan predicts the skills gap will grow to 1.8 million workers by 2022.

Too many alerts, too little time

In tandem with the lack of available personnel, incident response teams are bombarded by an unmanageable number of alerts. According to the Ponemon "Cost of Malware Containment" report, security teams can expect to log almost 17,000 malware alerts in a typical week. That's more than 100 alerts per hour for a team that operates 24/7. And those are only the alerts from malware incidents.

To put these figures in perspective, all these alerts can lead security teams to spend over 21,000 man-hours each year chasing down false positives. That's 2,625 standard eight-hour shifts needed just to distinguish bad alerts from good ones.

Time to response is rising

When you have too few skilled personnel and too many alerts, there's only one outcome: the time to resolve genuine security incidents will rise. According to analysis of source data from a recent Verizon Data Breach Investigations Report, while median time to incident detection is a fairly reasonable four hours, median time to resolution (MTTR) is more than four days.

Of course, cybercriminals have no such time constraints. Once they gain a foothold inside a target network, time to compromise is usually measured in minutes. We will discuss this more in Chapter 4.

A piecemeal approach

Most organizations' security groups have grown organically in parallel with increases in cyber risk. As a result, they have added security technologies and processes piecemeal, without a strategic design.

While this ad hoc approach is perfectly normal, it forces incident response teams to spend a lot of time aggregating data and context from a variety of security technologies (e.g., SIEM, EDR, and firewall logs) and threat feeds. This effort significantly extends response times and increases the likelihood that mistakes will be made.

 ON THE WEB You can find the original "Cost of Malware Containment" report on the Ponemon website.

The Reactivity Problem

Once an alert is flagged, it must be triaged, remediated, and followed up as quickly as possible to minimize cyber risk.

Consider a typical incident response process:

1. **Incident detection** — Receive an alert from a SIEM, EDR, or similar product.
2. **Discovery** — Determine what's happened and how to respond.
3. **Triage and containment** — Take immediate actions to mitigate the threat and minimize damage.
4. **Remediation** — Repair damage and remove infections.
5. **Push to BAU** — Pass the incident to "business as usual" teams for final actions.

Notice how reactive this process is. For most organizations, nearly all the work necessary to remediate an incident is back-loaded, meaning it can't be completed until after an alert is flagged. Although this is inevitable to some degree, it is far from ideal when incident response teams are already struggling to resolve incidents quickly enough.

Minimizing Reactivity in Incident Response

To reduce response times, incident response teams must become less reactive. Two areas where advanced preparation can be especially helpful are identification of probable threats and prioritization.

Identification of probable threats

If an incident response team can identify the most commonly faced threats in advance, they can develop strong, consistent processes to cope with them. This preparation dramatically reduces the time the team needs to contain individual incidents, prevents mistakes, and frees up analysts to cope with new and unexpected threats when they arise.

Prioritization

Not all threats are equal. If incident response teams can understand which threat vectors pose the greatest level of risk to their organization, they can allocate their time and resources accordingly.

ON THE WEB To find out how security experts use threat intelligence to reduce reactivity in incident response, watch the joint Recorded Future and LIFARS webinar "Fuel Incident Response With Threat Intelligence to Lower Breach Impact."

Strengthening Incident Response With Threat Intelligence

It should be clear from our discussion so far that *security technologies by themselves can't do enough to reduce pressure on human analysts.*

Threat intelligence can minimize the pressure on incident response teams and address many of the issues we have been reviewing by:

- ☑ Automatically identifying and dismissing false positive alerts
- ☑ Enriching alerts with real-time context from across the open and dark web
- ☑ Assembling and comparing information from internal and external data sources to identify genuine threats
- ☑ Scoring threats according to the organization's specific needs and infrastructure

In other words, threat intelligence provides incident response teams with exactly the actionable insights they need to make faster, better decisions, while holding back the tide of irrelevant and unreliable alerts that typically make their job so difficult.

Threat Intelligence in Action

Let's look at three use cases and one abuse case that show how threat intelligence affects incident response teams in the real world.

Use case: Prepare processes in advance

As we noted earlier, typical incident response processes are highly reactive, with most activity happening only after an incident occurs. This extends the time needed to scope and remediate incidents.

Threat intelligence can help incident response teams prepare for threats in advance by providing:

- ☑ A comprehensive, up-to-date picture of the threat landscape
- ☑ Information about popular threat actor tactics, techniques, and procedures (TTPs)
- ☑ Highlights of industry- and area-specific attack trends

Using this intelligence, incident response teams can develop and maintain strong processes for the most common incidents and threats. Having these processes available speeds up incident discovery, triage, and containment. It also greatly improves the consistency and reliability of actions across the incident response function.

Use case: Scope and contain incidents

When an incident occurs, incident response analysts must determine:

1. What happened
2. What the incident might mean for the organization
3. Which actions to take

All three of these factors must be analyzed as quickly as possible with a high degree of accuracy. Threat intelligence can help by:

☑ Automatically dismissing false positives, enabling teams to focus on genuine security incidents

☑ Enriching incidents with related information from across the open and dark web, making it easier to determine how much of a threat they pose and how the organization might be affected

☑ Providing details about the threat and insights about the attacker TTPs, helping the team make fast and effective containment and remediation decisions

Is Time Your Friend or Enemy?

Ever wondered how the balance of power fluctuates between attackers and defenders as time goes by? To find out, read the Recorded Future blog post "The 4th in the 5th: Temporal Aspects of Cyber Operations" by the grugq.

Use case: Remediate data exposure and stolen assets

It's common for organizations to take a long time to realize a breach has occurred. According to the "Ponemon 2018 Cost of a Data Breach Study," organizations in the United States take an average of 196 days to detect a breach.

Not surprisingly, stolen data and proprietary assets often turn up for sale on the dark web before their rightful owners realize what's happened.

A powerful threat intelligence capability can be a tremendous advantage. It can alert you to a breach by providing early warning that:

☑ Your assets are exposed online

☑ Someone is offering your assets for sale

Obtaining this intelligence in real time is vital because it will enable you to contain the incident as quickly as possible and help you identify when and how your network was breached.

Abuse case: Half measures are worse than nothing

We want to caution you about one "abuse case" where threat intelligence can actually undermine incident response.

At the start of their threat intelligence journey, some organizations opt for a minimalist solution such as a threat intelligence solution paired with a variety of free threat feeds. They might believe that this "dip the toes in the water" approach will minimize up-front costs.

While this type of implementation arms incident response teams with some actionable intelligence, it usually makes things worse by forcing analysts to wade through vast quantities of false positives and irrelevant alerts. To fully address the primary incident response pain points, a threat intelligence capability must be comprehensive, relevant, contextualized, and integrated.

Essential Characteristics of Threat Intelligence for Incident Response

Now it's time for us to examine the characteristics of a powerful threat intelligence capability, and how they address the greatest pain points of incident response teams.

Comprehensive

To be valuable to incident response teams, threat intelligence must be captured automatically from the widest possible range of locations across open sources, technical feeds, and the dark web. Otherwise analysts will be forced to conduct their own manual research to ensure nothing important has been missed.

TECH TALK

Imagine an analyst needs to know whether an IP address has been associated with malicious activity. If she is confident that her threat intelligence has been drawn from a comprehensive range of threat sources, she can query the data instantly and be sure the result will be accurate. If she isn't confident, she will have to spend time manually checking the IP address against several threat data sources. Figure 3-1 shows how threat intelligence might connect an IP address with the Trickbot malware. This kind of intelligence can be correlated with internal network logs to reveal indicators of compromise.

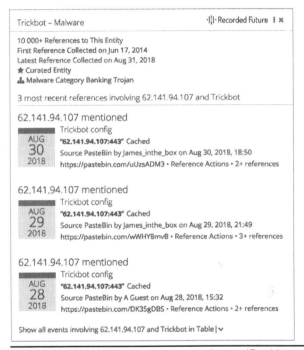

Figure 3-1: Threat intelligence connecting an IP address with the Trickbot malware. (Source: Recorded Future)

ON THE WEB

While they are often used interchangeably, threat intelligence, information, and data aren't the same thing. To find out where the differences lie, read the Recorded Future blog post "Threat Intelligence, Information, and Data: What Is the Difference?"

Relevant

It's impossible to avoid all false positives when working to identify and contain incidents. But threat intelligence should help incident response teams quickly identify and purge false positives generated by security technologies such as SIEM and EDR products.

There are two categories of false positives to consider:

1. Alerts that are relevant to an organization but are inaccurate or unhelpful

2. Alerts that are accurate and/or interesting but *aren't* relevant to the organization

Both types have the potential to waste an enormous amount of incident response analysts' time.

Advanced threat intelligence products are now employing machine learning technology to identify and discard false positives automatically and draw analysts' attention to the most important (i.e., most relevant) intelligence.

CAUTION

If you don't choose your threat intelligence technology carefully, your team can waste a great deal of time on intelligence that's inaccurate, outdated, or irrelevant to your organization.

Contextualized

Not all threats are created equal. Even among relevant threat alerts, some will inevitably be more urgent and important than the rest. An alert from a single source could be both accurate and relevant, but still not particularly high in priority. That is why context is so important: it provides critical clues about which alerts are most likely to be significant to your organization.

Contextual information related to an alert might include:

☑ Corroboration from multiple sources that the same type of alert has been associated with recent attacks

☑ Confirmation that it has been associated with threat actors known to be active in your industry

☑ A timeline showing that the alert occurred slightly before or after other events linked with attacks

Modern machine learning and artificial intelligence (AI) technologies make it possible for a threat intelligence solution to consider multiple sources concurrently and determine which alerts are most important to a specific organization.

Integrated

Among the most critical functions of a threat intelligence system is the ability to integrate with a broad range of security tools, including SIEM and incident response solutions, examine the alerts they generate, and:

- ☑ Determine whether each alert should be dismissed as a false positive
- ☑ Score the alert according to its importance
- ☑ Enrich the alert with valuable extra context

This integration eliminates the need for analysts to manually compare each alert to information in diverse security and threat intelligence tools. Even more important, integration and automated processes can filter out a huge number of false positives *without any checking by a human analyst.* The amount of time and frustration this capability saves makes it perhaps the single greatest benefit of threat intelligence for incident response teams.

Chapter 4

Threat Intelligence for Vulnerability Management

- Examine the current challenges in addressing vulnerabilities based on actual risk
- Learn how vulnerability intelligence delivers insights into threat actor behaviors
- See how risk-based intelligence streamlines the operational elements of vulnerability management

"The acknowledgment of our weakness is the first step in repairing our loss."

— Thomas à Kempis

Vulnerability management is not glamorous, but it is one of the very few ways you can be proactive in securing your organization. Its importance as a function cannot be overstated.

The key to success in vulnerability management is to shift the thinking of your security teams from trying to patch everything to making risk-based decisions. That is critical because the vast ocean of vulnerabilities disclosed each year stretches to the breaking point the teams responsible for identifying vulnerable assets and deploying patches. And the key to making good risk-based decisions is taking advantage of more sources of threat intelligence.

The Vulnerability Problem by the Numbers

According to research from the analyst firm Gartner, Inc., about 8,000 vulnerabilities a year were disclosed over the past decade. The number rose only slightly from year to year, and only about one in eight were actually exploited. However, during the same period, the amount of new software coming into use grew immensely, and the number of threats has increased exponentially.

In other words, although the number of breaches and threats has increased over the past 10 years, only a small percentage were based on new vulnerabilities. As Gartner put it, "More threats are leveraging the same small set of vulnerabilities."

Zero day does not mean top priority

Zero-day threats regularly draw an outsize amount of attention. However, the vast majority of "new" threats labeled as zero day are actually variations on a theme, exploiting the same old vulnerabilities in slightly different ways. Further, the data shows that the number of vulnerabilities actually exploited on day zero make up only about 0.4 percent of all vulnerabilities exploited during the last decade.

The implication is that the most effective approach to vulnerability management is not to focus on zero-day threats, but rather to identify and patch the vulnerabilities specific to the software your organization uses.

Time is of the essence

Threat actors have gotten quicker at exploiting vulnerabilities. According to Gartner, the average time it takes between the identification of a vulnerability and the appearance of an exploit in the wild has dropped from 45 days to 15 days over the last decade.

This has two implications:

1. You have roughly two weeks to patch or remediate your systems against a new exploit.
2. If you can't patch in that timeframe, you should have a plan to mitigate the damage.

Research from IBM X-Force shows that if a vulnerability is not exploited within two weeks to three months after it is announced, it is statistically unlikely that it ever will be. Therefore "old" vulnerabilities are usually not a priority for patching.

ON THE WEB

Exploits usually target the most widely used technologies. An episode of the Recorded Future podcast entitled "7 of the Top 10 Vulnerabilities Target Microsoft" explains why.

DON'T FORGET

All of these statistics point to one conclusion: your goal should not be to patch the most vulnerabilities, or even the most zero-day threats, but rather to identify and address the threats most likely to be exploited against your organization.

Assess Risk Based on Exploitability

Let's use a metaphor: if patching vulnerabilities to keep your network safe is like getting vaccines to protect yourself from disease, then you need to decide which vaccinations are priorities and which are unnecessary. You may need a flu shot every season to stay healthy, but there's no need to stay vaccinated against yellow fever or malaria unless you will be exposed to them.

That's why you have to do your research: one of the greatest values of a threat intelligence solution is that it identifies the specific vulnerabilities that represent risk to your organization and gives you visibility into their likelihood of exploitation.

Figure 4-1 illustrates the point. Out of the thousands of vulnerabilities that are currently disclosed, hundreds are being exploited. And it's true that at least some of those vulnerabilities probably exist in your environment. But the only ones you really need to worry about are those that lie within the intersection of those two categories.

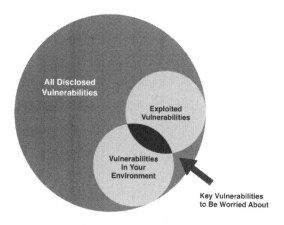

Figure 4-1: The biggest risks are vulnerabilities that are present in your organization and currently being exploited. (Source: Gartner)

Severity ratings can be misleading

A common mistake in managing vulnerabilities is to focus on ranking threats in terms of severity. Ranking and classification systems like Common Vulnerabilities and Exposures (CVE) naming and Common Vulnerability Scoring Systems (CVSSs) don't take into account whether threat actors are actually exploiting vulnerabilities right now in your industry or locations. Relying solely on vulnerability severity is like getting a vaccine for the bubonic plague before a flu shot because the plague killed more people at some point in history.

The Genesis of Threat Intelligence: Vulnerability Databases

Vulnerability databases consolidate information on disclosed vulnerabilities and also score their exploitability.

In fact, one of the very first forms of threat intelligence was NIST's National Vulnerability Database (NVD). It centralized information on disclosed vulnerabilities to help make it easier for organizations to see if they were likely to be affected. For more than 20 years, the NVD has collected information on more than 100,000 vulnerabilities, making it an invaluable source for information security professionals. Other nations, including China and Russia, have followed NIST's lead by setting up vulnerability databases.

 ON THE WEB You can find the NIST NVD at https://nvd.nist.gov/. A catalog of vulnerability databases is published by the industry organization FIRST: https://www.first.org/global/sigs/vrdx/vdb-catalog.

However, there are two significant limitations to most vulnerability databases:

1. They focus on technical exploitability rather than active exploitation.

1. They are not updated fast enough to provide warning of some quickly spreading threats.

Exploitability versus exploitation

Information in the vulnerability databases is almost entirely focused on technical exploitability, a judgment of how likely it is that exploiting a particular vulnerability will result in greater or lesser damage to systems and networks. In the NVD, this is measured through the CVSS scoring system.

But technical exploitability and active exploitation are not the same thing. CVSS base scores provide a metric that's reasonably accurate and easy to understand — provided you know what information the score is conveying. But unless a base score is modified by a temporal score or an environmental score, it really only tells you how bad the vulnerability is *hypothetically*, not whether it's actually being exploited in the wild.

Figure 4-2 shows the kind of threat intelligence available about a vulnerability and the risk it poses. In this case you can also see how reports involving the CVE are appearing before it has been given a CVSS score by NVD.

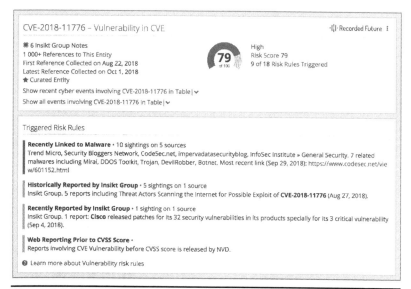

Figure 4-2: Threat intelligence related to a vulnerability. (Source: Recorded Future)

TECH TALK

An object lesson in the difference between the NVD's "official risk" and "real risk" from a vulnerability in the wild is CVE-2017-0022. Despite its having a CVSS severity score of only 4.3 (in the medium range), Recorded Future recently included it in a list of the top 10 vulnerabilities used by cybercriminals. The real risk is very high because threat actors have added this vulnerability to the widespread Neutrino Exploit Kit, where it performs a critical role checking whether security software is installed on a target system.

Next week versus now

Another shortcoming of many vulnerability databases is lack of timeliness. For example, 75 percent of disclosed vulnerabilities appear on other online sources before they appear in the NVD, and on average it takes those vulnerabilities a week to show up there. This is a very serious problem, because it handicaps security teams in the race to patch before adversaries can exploit, as illustrated in Figure 4-3.

TECH TALK

The informal way in which vulnerabilities are disclosed and announced contributes to the delay in recognizing them in vulnerability databases. Typically, a vendor or researcher discloses the vulnerability to the NVD, which assigns a CVE and begins an analysis. In the meantime, the vendor or researcher publishes more information on its own blog or a social media account. Good luck collating data from these disparate and hard-to-find sources before criminal actors develop proof-of-concept malware and add it to exploit kits!

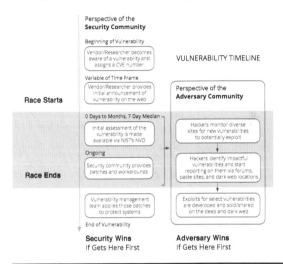

Figure 4-3: The race between security professionals and adversaries.

ON THE WEB For research on the lag in reporting vulnerabilities and its implications, see the Recorded Future blog post "The Race Between Security Professionals and Adversaries."

Threat Intelligence and Real Risk

The most effective way to assess the true risk of a vulnerability to your organization is to combine:

- ☑ Internal vulnerability scanning data

- ☑ External intelligence from a breadth of sources

- ☑ An understanding of why threat actors are targeting certain vulnerabilities and ignoring others

Internal vulnerability scanning

Almost every vulnerability management team scans their internal systems for vulnerabilities, correlates the results with information reported in vulnerability databases, and uses the result to determine what should be patched. This is a basic use of operational threat intelligence, even if we don't usually think of it that way.

Conventional scanning is an excellent way to *de-prioritize* vulnerabilities that don't appear on your systems. By itself, however, scanning is not an adequate way to accurately prioritize vulnerabilities that are found.

Risk milestones for vulnerabilities

One powerful way to assess the risk of a vulnerability is to look at how far it has progressed from initial identification to availability, weaponization, and commoditization in exploit kits.

The level of real risk rises dramatically as it passes through the milestones shown in Figure 4-4. Broad-based threat intelligence can reveal the progress of a vulnerability along this path.

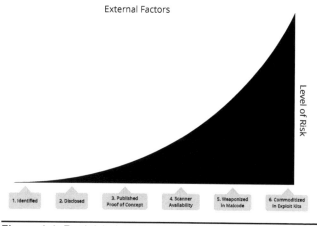

Figure 4-4: Real risk rises dramatically when vulnerabilities progress to weaponization and commoditization.

Understanding the adversary

As discussed elsewhere in this book, good threat intelligence should not simply provide information in the form of scores and statistics, but also a deeper understanding of how and why threat actors are targeting certain vulnerabilities and ignoring others. Below we discuss sources of intelligence that can contribute to this understanding.

How to Create Meaningful Risk Scores

What factors beyond technical characteristics can be used to calculate risk scores of vulnerabilities? Recorded Future's native risk scoring system incorporates data about criminal adoption, patterns in exploit sharing, and the number of links to malware. This information often comes from sources that are difficult to access, like forums on the dark web.

Sources of Intelligence

Data from asset scans and external vulnerability databases are only the starting points for information that can help you assess the risk of vulnerabilities. Threat intelligence should include data from a wide range of sources, or analysts risk missing emerging vulnerabilities until it's too late.

Valuable sources of information for assessing true risk to your business include:

- ☑ **Information security sites**, including vendor blogs, official disclosure information on vulnerabilities, and security news sites

- ☑ **Social media**, where link sharing provides jumping-off points for uncovering useful intelligence

- ☑ **Code repositories** such as GitHub, which yield insights into the development of proof-of-concept code for vulnerabilities

- ☑ **Paste sites** such as Pastebin and Ghostbin (sometimes wrongly defined as dark web locations), which often house lists of exploitable vulnerabilities

- ☑ **The dark web**, composed of communities and marketplaces with a bar to entry where exploits are developed, shared, and sold

☑ **Forums** with no bar to entry or requirement to be using specific software, where threat actors exchange information on vulnerabilities and exploits

☑ **Technical feeds**, which deliver data streams of potentially malicious indicators that add useful context around the activities of malware and exploit kits

---

Vulnerability Chatter on the Dark Web

It's not easy to eavesdrop on the channels through which threat actors communicate and operate:

- Underground forums are difficult to find (after all, there's no Google for the dark web).

- Threat actors change locations whenever they feel their anonymity is at risk.

- Finding the crumb that might be relevant to your security is no small endeavor.

- There are likely to be bars to entry, either financial or kudos from the rest of the community.

- Many of these forums operate exclusively in local languages.

Threat intelligence vendors with expertise in collecting and analyzing dark web intelligence come into play here. They can provide you with contextualized information from dark web forums on vulnerabilities directly relevant to your network.

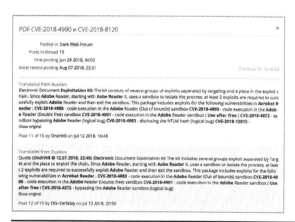

Figure 4-5: A post in a dark web forum shows threat actors exchanging information. (Source: Recorded Future)

Use Case: Cross-Referencing Intelligence

To accurately assess real risk, you must be able to correlate information from multiple threat intelligence sources. Once you begin to understand how individual references combine to tell the whole story, you will be able to map the intelligence you have to the risk milestones a vulnerability typically goes through.

For example, you might notice a new vulnerability disclosed on a vendor's website. Then you discover a tweet with a link to proof-of-concept code on GitHub. Later you find exploit code is being sold on a dark web forum. Eventually you might see news reports of the vulnerability being exploited in the wild.

TIP
This kind of intelligence can help you narrow your focus to vulnerabilities that truly present the greatest risk and move away from a "race to patch everything" mode of operation.

Bridging the Risk Gaps Between Security, Operations, and Business Leadership

In most organizations, the responsibility for protecting against vulnerabilities devolves onto two teams:

1. The vulnerability management team runs scans and prioritizes vulnerabilities by potential risk.
2. The IT operations team deploys patches and remediates the affected systems.

This dynamic creates a tendency to approach vulnerability management "by the numbers." For example, the vulnerability management team in the security organization might determine that several vulnerabilities in Apache web servers pose a very high risk to the business and should be given top priority. However, the IT operations team may be supporting a lot more Windows systems than Apache servers. If team members are measured strictly on the number of systems patched, they have an incentive to keep their focus on lower-priority Windows vulnerabilities.

Intelligence on exploitability also prepares your organization to strike the correct balance between patching vulnerable systems and interrupting business operations. Most organizations have a strong aversion to disturbing business continuity. But if you know that a patch will protect the organization against a real, imminent risk, then a short interruption is completely justified.

The risk milestones framework outlined above makes it much easier to communicate the danger of a vulnerability across your security and operations teams, up through senior managers, and even to the board. This level of visibility into the rationale behind decisions made around vulnerabilities will increase confidence in the security team across your entire organization.

TIP To reduce the gap between the vulnerability management and IT operations teams, introduce risk of exploitability. Arm the vulnerability management team with more contextualized data about the risk of exploitability so they can pinpoint a smaller number of high-risk CVEs and make fewer demands on the operations team. The operations team can then give first priority to that small number of critical patches and still have time to address other goals.

Chapter 5

Threat Intelligence for Security Leaders

In this chapter

- See how threat intelligence supports risk management and targeted investment in cybersecurity programs
- Explore the types of threat intelligence CISOs find most valuable
- Review how threat intelligence helps mitigate the security skills gap

"An investment in knowledge pays the best interest."

— Benjamin Franklin

The job of the CISO has seen dramatic shifts in recent years. It once centered on making decisions about purchasing and implementing security technologies. Now CISOs are far more likely to interact with the CEO and the board and to perform delicate balancing acts of pre-empting risk while ensuring business continuity.

Today, security leaders must:

☑ Assess business and technical risks, including emerging threats and "known unknowns" that might impact the business

☑ Identify the right strategies and technologies to mitigate the risks

☑ Communicate the nature of the risks to top management and justify investments in defensive measures

Threat intelligence can be a critical resource for all these activities.

Risk Management

Perhaps the greatest responsibility of the modern CISO is risk management: taking the resources and budget available and allocating them in a way that most efficiently mitigates the threat of cyber incidents and attacks. Figure 5-1 outlines the stages security leaders move through when approaching this challenge.

Assess Security Requirements	Understand business and IT objectives and define responsibilities for the security function.
Assess Existing Security Protocols	Analyze current security people, processes, and technologies to develop an accurate picture of the security function.
Develop Initiatives	Using a risk-based approach, identify the most significant gaps in security, then define and prioritize initiatives to address them.
Plan the Transition	Continually monitor progress and ensure the security function is improving in line with requirements. Develop metrics to measure ongoing effectiveness.

Figure 5-1: A standard approach to assessing risk and developing a security strategy.

Internal data is not enough

The approach to security outlined in Figure 5-1 depends on having good information about relevant risk factors and potential weaknesses in existing security programs. The problem is that too often this kind of intelligence is only gathered from internal audits, known issues, and previous security incidents. That produces a list of problems you already know about, not a list of the problems you need to worry about today or in the future.

External context is needed to verify risk related to known problems and provide warning about emerging and unforeseen threats.

Internal network traffic data, event logs, and alerting obviously bring value to risk management, but they don't provide enough context to build a comprehensive risk profile, and certainly not enough to define an entire strategy. Security professionals must be proactive about uncovering unknown risks. Context is what helps security leaders determine which potential threats are most likely to become actual threats to their enterprise.

Sharpening the focus

Threat intelligence includes information on general trends such as:

☑ Which types of attacks are becoming more (or less) frequent

☑ Which types of attacks are most costly to the victims

☑ What new kinds of threat actors are coming forward, and which assets and enterprises are they targeting

☑ The security practices and technologies that have proven the most (or least) successful in stopping or mitigating these attacks

Data on these trends can help security organizations anticipate which threats will be the hot news items of tomorrow.

But contextualized external threat intelligence can go much further, enabling security groups to assess whether an emerging threat is likely to affect their specific enterprise based on factors like:

☑ **Industry**: Is the threat affecting other businesses in our vertical?

☑ **Technology**: Does the threat involve compromising software, hardware, or other technologies used in our enterprise?

☑ **Geography**: Does the threat target facilities in regions where we have operations?

☑ **Attack method**: Have techniques used in the attack, including social engineering and technical methods, been used successfully against our company or similar ones?

Without these types of intelligence, gathered from an extremely broad set of external data sources, it is impossible for security decision makers to obtain a holistic view of the cyber risk landscape and the greatest risks to their enterprise.

Figure 5-2 illustrates how a customized threat intelligence dashboard can highlight intelligence that is most relevant to a specific enterprise.

Figure 5-2: A threat intelligence dashboard can pinpoint threats most relevant to a specific industry or technology. (Source: Recorded Future)

Mitigation: People, Processes, and Tools

Vulnerability scans and techniques such as penetration testing and red teaming can help security organizations understand where gaps exist in their defenses.

But today's enterprises have far more technical vulnerabilities, more weaknesses in security processes and policies, and more employees susceptible to social engineering techniques than they can possibly patch, harden, and train in the immediate future.

Threat intelligence helps security leaders pinpoint the vulnerabilities and weaknesses that need to be addressed first by indicating:

☑ Which threat actors are most likely to target the enterprise

☑ The TTPs those threat actors use, and therefore the weaknesses they tend to exploit

Early warnings

Sometimes threat intelligence can be even more specific. For example, analysts have found hackers on the dark web announcing their intention to attack specific industries, and even specific companies (sometimes to recruit like-minded hackers to assist them).

Analysts monitoring dark web marketplaces can also track the development and sale of hacker tools and exploit kits targeting specific vulnerabilities. As discussed earlier in this book, it is important to patch vulnerabilities and mitigate weaknesses that are at the point of being exploited before tackling others where exploitation is theoretical.

 TIP

You can use some threat intelligence solutions to scan the dark web and other sources for references to your company, your industry, and specific technologies installed in your enterprise.

Investment

Deciding how to invest in cybersecurity has become a daunting challenge in recent times. Financial investment advisers Momentum Partners identified more than 1,700 companies in 2017 that specialize in cybersecurity technologies and services. With so many choices, how can CISOs identify the most effective solutions to implement as part of a proactive security strategy?

The only logical way is to make investment decisions based on risk. Each organization has its own unique risk profile, shaped by its industry, locations, and internal infrastructure. Threat intelligence helps security leaders understand their organization's most pressing threats, making the task of identifying (and justifying) areas for investment much simpler. The end goal is to be able to judge that risk and make investments based upon sound knowledge of the true threat landscape.

Communication

CISOs are often challenged by the need to describe threats and justify countermeasures in terms that will motivate non-technical business leaders, such as cost, ROI, impact on customers, and competitive advantages.

Bombarding them with news about every single threat is not a good option.

Threat intelligence can provide powerful ammunition for these discussions, such as:

☑ The impact of similar attacks on companies of the same size in other industries

☑ Trends and intelligence from the dark web indicating that the enterprise is likely to be targeted

Supporting Security Leaders

We have mentioned several times that threat intelligence needs to be comprehensive, relevant, and contextualized to be useful to members of the security organization. When it comes to CISOs and other security leaders, it also needs to be concise and timely.

For example, threat intelligence can provide security leaders with a real-time picture of the latest threats, trends, and events. A threat intelligence dashboard or some other type of "at-a-glance" format can help security leaders respond to a threat or communicate the potential impact of a new threat type to business leaders and board members.

DON'T FORGET

Threat intelligence is not just for incident response teams and SOCs. Security leaders are also key consumers of threat intelligence, as illustrated in Figure 1-1. Think through the kinds of intelligence security leaders need on a daily basis (say, a dashboard and a list of key new intelligence findings from the previous day), at regular intervals (summaries and trends for a quarterly risk report), and for crises (intelligence about attacks that have just been detected), and make sure processes and threat intelligence tools are in place to address these needs.

The Security Skills Gap

One of the responsibilities of a CISO is to make sure the IT organization has the human resources to carry out its mission. Yet the cybersecurity field has a widely publicized skills shortage, and existing security staff frequently find themselves under pressure to cope with unmanageable workloads.

Threat intelligence can provide a partial answer to that crisis by automating some of the most labor-intensive tasks in cybersecurity and freeing people's time for other tasks. For example, it can reduce the massive volume of alerts generated by SIEMs and other security tools, rapidly collect and correlate context from multiple intelligence sources, and provide data to prioritize risks.

A threat intelligence solution made available across the security function can save a huge amount of time, as SOC and incident response analysts, vulnerability management specialists, and other security personnel are given the information and context they need to make accurate decisions.

Powerful threat intelligence also helps junior personnel quickly "upskill" and perform above their experience level, so the CISO doesn't have to recruit as many senior staff.

Intelligence to Manage Better

It's clear that the greatest challenge for CISOs and other security leaders is how to balance limited resources against the need to secure their organizations against ever-evolving cyber threats. Threat intelligence addresses these issues by helping them to build a picture of the threat landscape, accurately calculate cyber risk, and arm security personnel with the intelligence and context they need to make better, faster decisions.

Threat intelligence enables CISOs and security leaders to stay abreast of current and emerging threats in a way that simply isn't possible through manual research. But for that to happen, a threat intelligence capability must be comprehensive, relevant, contextualized, concise, and timely. Threat intelligence capabilities without these characteristics will most likely hinder more than help, as partial or inaccurate information can easily lead to poor decision making.

Case Study: Threat Intelligence and Automation at a Global Retailer

With nearly 3,600 stores and over 135,000 employees worldwide, the chain's security challenges run the gamut from loss prevention, fraud, and corporate security to protecting customers' PII.

The retailer applies automation to both centralizing and customizing threat intelligence for every security function. Automation ensures that data going into its SIEM is accurate and highly contextual, and that the data coming out is in flexible, easy-to-use formats.

The biggest return on investment — and the biggest advantage to managing its threat intelligence through an all-in-one platform — is

better relationships both across the cybersecurity teams and with other departments in the organization.

Says a senior manager at the company's Cyber Defense Center: "None of us is operating in a silo. If we can use threat intelligence to keep us safe, but also help our program visibility, that helps to make a business case for more capabilities. Having champions on other teams to back the benefits of threat intelligence really helps our return on investment."

Read the full case study or watch the webinar at https://www.recordedfuture.com/gap-threat-intelligence-needs/.

Chapter 6

Threat Intelligence for Risk Analysis

- Explore the value of risk models like the FAIR framework
- See right and wrong ways to gather data about risk
- Learn how threat intelligence can provide hard data about attack probabilities and costs

---

"Establish and promote information risk management best practices that ...[achieve] the right balance between protecting the organization and running the business."

— Mission statement of the FAIR Institute

As we mentioned in the previous chapter, today there are more than 1,700 vendors in cybersecurity. Most of them define their mission as some version of "making your environment secure." But how can enterprises set priorities for investing in technology and services, as well as people?

Risk modeling offers a way to objectively assess current risks, and to estimate clear and quantifiable outcomes from investments in cybersecurity. But many cyber risk models today suffer from either:

☑   Vague, non-quantified output, often in the form of "stoplight charts" that show green, yellow, and red threat levels

☑   Estimates about threat probabilities and costs that are hastily compiled, based on partial information, and riddled with unfounded assumptions

Non-quantified output is not very actionable, while models based on faulty input result in "garbage in-garbage out" scenarios, whose output appears to be precise but is in fact misleading.

To avoid these problems, enterprises need a well-designed risk model and plenty of valid, current information, including threat intelligence.

TIP Cybersecurity risk assessments should not be based only on criteria defined to prove compliance with regulations. With those criteria, assessing risk usually becomes an exercise in checking boxes against cybersecurity controls like firewalls and encryption. Counting the number of boxes checked gives you a very misleading picture of actual risk.

The FAIR Risk Model

The type of equation at the core of any risk model is:

"Likelihood of occurrence x impact"

But clearly God (or the Devil) is in the details. Fortunately, some smart people have developed some very good risk models and methodologies that you can use or adapt to your own needs. One that we like is the Factor Analysis of Information Risk (FAIR) model from the FAIR Institute. Figure 6-1 shows the framework of this model.

The FAIR framework helps you create a quantitative risk assessment model that contains specific probabilities for loss from specific kinds of threats.

ON THE WEB You can learn more about FAIR at the FAIR Institute website. This quantitative model for information security and operational risk is focused on understanding, analyzing, and quantifying information risk in real financial terms.

Figure 6-1: The FAIR Framework, with elements informed by intelligence highlighted. (Source: The FAIR Institute)

Measurements and transparency are key

The FAIR framework (and others like it) enable you to create risk models that:

☑ Make defined measurements of risk

☑ Are transparent about assumptions, variables, and outcomes

☑ Show specific loss probabilities in financial terms

When measurements, formulas, assumptions, variables, and outcomes are made transparent, they can be discussed, defended, and changed. Because much of the FAIR model is defined in business and financial terms, executives, line of business managers, and other stakeholders can learn to speak the same language and to classify assets, threats, and vulnerabilities in the same way.

TIP Try to incorporate specific probabilities about future losses into your risk model whenever possible. Specific probabilities enable risk managers and senior executives to discuss the model and how it can be improved, after which they have more confidence in the model and the recommendations that come out of it.

Which Statement Is More Useful?

"The threat from DDoS attacks to our business has been changed from high to medium (red to yellow)."

Or

"There is a 20 percent probability that our business will incur a loss of over $300,000 in the next 12 months because a distributed denial-of-service (DDoS) attack will disrupt the availability of our customer-facing websites."

"The threat of ransomware to our business has changed from low to medium (green to yellow)."

Or

"There is a 10 percent probability that our business will incur a loss of $150,000 in the next 12 months due to ransomware."

Threat Intelligence and Threat Probabilities

As shown in the left side of Figure 6-1, a big part of creating a threat model involves estimating the probability of successful attacks (or "loss event frequency" in the language of the FAIR framework).

The first step is to create a list of threat categories that might affect the business. This list typically includes malware, phishing attacks, exploit kits, zero-day attacks, web application exploits, DDoS attacks, ransomware, and many other threats.

The next step is much more difficult: to estimate probabilities that the attacks will happen, and that they will succeed (i.e., the odds that the enterprise contains vulnerabilities related to the attacks and existing controls are not sufficient to stop them).

TIP Try to avoid the following scenario: A GRC (governance, risk, and compliance) team member asks a security analyst, "What is the likelihood of our facing this particular attack?" The security analyst (who really can't win) thinks for 30 seconds about past experience and current security controls and makes a wild guess: "I dunno, maybe 20 percent."

To avoid appearing clueless, your security team needs answers that are better informed than that one. Threat intelligence can help by answering questions such as:

- ☑ Which threat actors are using this attack, and do they target our industry?
- ☑ How often has this specific attack been observed recently by enterprises like ours?
- ☑ Is the trend up or down?
- ☑ Which vulnerabilities does this attack exploit (and are those vulnerabilities present in our enterprise)?
- ☑ What kind of damage, technical and financial, has this attack caused in enterprises like ours?

Analysts still need to know a great deal about the enterprise and its security defenses, but threat intelligence enriches their knowledge of attacks, the actors behind them, and their targets. It also provides hard data on the prevalence of the attacks.

Figures 6-2 and 6-3 show some of the forms the intelligence might take. Figure 6-2 lists the kinds of questions about a malware sample that a threat intelligence solution can answer for analysts.

Figure 6-2: Questions about a malware sample that a threat intelligence solution can answer. (Source: Recorded Future)

Figure 6-3 shows trends in the proliferation of ransomware families. The trend line to the right of each ransomware family indicates increasing or decreasing references across a huge range of threat data sources such as code repositories, paste sites, security research blogs, criminal forums, and .onion (Tor accessible) forums. Additional information might be available about how the ransomware families connect to threat actors, targets, and exploit kits.

Figure 6-3: Timeline depicting the proliferation of new ransomware families. (Source: Recorded Future)

Threat Intelligence and the Cost of Attacks

The other major component of the formulas in our model is the probable cost of successful attacks. Most of the data for estimating cost is likely to come from inside the enterprise. However, threat intelligence can provide useful reference points on topics like:

- ☑ The cost of similar attacks on enterprises of the same size and in the same industry
- ☑ The systems that need to be remediated after an attack, and the type of remediation they require

Go Deeper on Risk

You can find out more about risk modeling and the role of threat intelligence by viewing the Recorded Future white paper "The Probability of Loss: How Threat Intelligence Quantifies Risk for the Business."

To go even deeper, we highly recommend "How to Measure Anything in Cybersecurity Risk" by Douglas W. Hubbard and Richard Seiersen.

Chapter 7

Threat Intelligence for Fraud Prevention

In this chapter

- Understand how cybercriminals organize themselves to execute fraud and extortion
- See how conversations in criminal communities present opportunities to gather valuable threat intelligence
- Learn which types of cyber fraud you can combat by applying relevant threat intelligence

"The challenge for capitalism is that the things that breed trust also breed the environment for fraud."

— James Surowiecki

Stand and Deliver!

Since the birth of commerce, criminals have looked for ways to make an easy profit from those in possession of assets and to make the most of technology available at the time. In 17th century England, for example, the growth in coach travel among an affluent merchant class, combined with the invention of the portable flintlock pistol, gave rise to the highwayman.

In our digital age, companies that transact business online find their data targeted by various forms of cyber fraud.

To understand how criminals are looking to profit from your business, you cannot focus solely on detecting and responding to threats already actively exploiting your systems. You need to gather threat intelligence about the cybercriminal gangs targeting you and how they run their operations.

Know Your Enemy

Verizon's 2018 Data Breach Investigations Report attributed more than 60 percent of confirmed breaches to organized crime (Figure 7-1).

This data aligns with intelligence gathered by Recorded Future from dark web communities showing that organized criminal groups (OCGs) are employing freelance hackers to defraud businesses and individuals. These groups operate just like legitimate businesses in many ways, with a hierarchy of members working as a team to create, operate, and maintain fraud schemes.

Top External Actor Varieties in Breaches

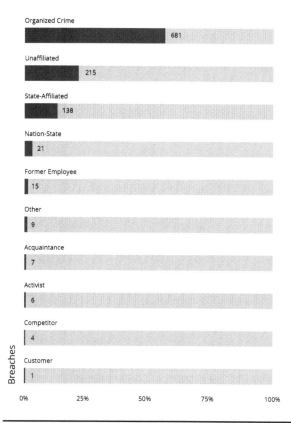

Figure 7-1: Top external actor varieties in data breaches. (Source: Verizon Data Breach Investigation Report 2018)

Figure 7-2: A typical organizational chart for a cybercrime syndicate. (Source: Recorded Future)

A typical OCG is controlled by a single mastermind. The group might include bankers with extensive connections in the financial industry to arrange money laundering, forgers responsible for fake documents and supporting paperwork, professional project managers who oversee the technical aspects of operations, software engineers who write code, and skilled hackers. Some groups include ex-law enforcement agents who gather information and run counterintelligence operations.

The members of these cybercriminal syndicates tend to have strong ties in real life, and often they are respected members of their social groups. They certainly don't regard themselves as ordinary street criminals. They rarely cross paths with everyday gangsters, preferring to remain in the shadows and avoid attention from law enforcement and local mafia branches. However, schemes that require large numbers of people, such as those that involve taking cash out of multiple automated teller machines simultaneously, can involve a chain of intermediaries who recruit and manage the "troopers" who do the leg work.

Criminal Communities and the Dark Web

Only rarely can you attribute a cyberattack to a single individual operating in isolation. Advanced attacks typically require a wide range of skills and tools, and an infrastructure capable of launching and supporting campaigns that utilize ransomware, phishing, and other technical devices and social engineering techniques.

Today, all those products and services can be purchased or rented for a price in a sophisticated underground economy. Cybercriminals, hackers, and their accomplices exchange information and carry out transactions related to illicit activities on the deep web (areas of the web that cannot be reached by search engines) and the dark web (areas that can only be accessed with special software and tools that mask the identity of visitors).

Gated communities

Not all cybercriminals operate exclusively in what would technically be referred to as the dark web. Some build communities based on a fairly standard discussion board, encrypted behind a login, and use technologies like Jabber and Telegram to conduct their business.

Prospective members of this underground network are vetted by active participants in the chat rooms and forums before they are accepted. They may have to pay an entrance fee, ranging from US$50 to $2,000 or more. One forum required prospective members to deposit over $100,000.

A strength — and a weakness

The dark web and criminal communities strengthen cybercriminals and OCGs by giving them access to information, tools, infrastructure, and contract services that multiply their power and reach. However, these communities are also a weakness because they can be monitored to provide threat intelligence that can be used to anticipate and defeat fraud schemes.

Know Your Dark Networks

You can gain a deeper understanding of how the criminal underground maintains a hierarchy of users in research from Recorded Future: "Dark Networks: Social Network Analysis of Dark Web Communities." We found that the dark web is organized in three distinct communities: low-tier underground forums, higher-tier dark web forums, and dark web markets. Analysis revealed that a significant group of actors are posting in both low-tier and higher-tier forums, showing a connection between these two communities. However, dark web markets are largely disconnected from these forums.

Connecting the Dots for Fraud Prevention

Threat intelligence gathered from underground criminal communities is a window into the motivations, methods, and tactics of threat actors, especially when this intelligence is correlated with information from the surface web, including technical feeds and indicators.

The power of truly contextualized threat intelligence is shown by how it can draw together data from a wide variety of sources and make connections between disparate pieces of information.

For example, the following contextual information might be used to turn news about a new malware variant into intelligence:

☑ Evidence that criminal groups are using this malware in the wild

☑ Reports that exploit kits using the malware are available for sale on the dark web

☑ Confirmation that vulnerabilities targeted by the exploit kits are present in your enterprise

TIP Monitor the dark web and criminal communities for direct mentions of your organization and assets. These mentions often indicate targeting or potential breaches. But also monitor mentions of your industry and other less specific terms that might point to your operations. Using threat intelligence to assess risk in this way will give you more confidence about your defenses and help you make better decisions.

Use case: Payment fraud

The term payment fraud encompasses a wide variety of techniques by which cybercriminals profit from compromised payment data. They can use phishing to collect card details. More-complex attacks can compromise ecommerce sites or point-of-sale systems to achieve the same goal. Once they have acquired card data, the criminals can resell it (often as packs of numbers) and walk away with their cut.

Threat intelligence can provide early warning of upcoming attacks related to payment fraud. Monitoring sources like criminal communities, paste sites, and other forums for relevant payment card numbers, bank identifier numbers, or specific references to financial institutions can give visibility into criminal operations that might affect your organization.

Use case: Compromised data

Other types of compromised personal information and corporate intellectual property also can have enormous intrinsic value. Recent examples include compromised medical records, cloned and compromised gift cards, and stolen credentials to "pay for" services like Netflix, Uber, and items charged via PayPal, as illustrated in Figure 7-3.

Figure 7-3: Compromised data – Spotify credentials disclosed on the dark web. (Source: Recorded Future)

A high percentage of hacking-related breaches leverage stolen or weak passwords. Cybercriminals regularly upload massive caches of usernames and passwords to paste sites and the dark web, or make them available for sale on underground marketplaces. These data dumps can include corporate email addresses and passwords, as well as login details for other sites.

Monitoring external sources for this type of intelligence will dramatically increase your visibility, not just into leaked credentials, but also into potential breaches of corporate data and proprietary code.

Use case: Typosquatting and fraudulent domains

Typosquatting involves manipulating the characters in a company's domain name into nearly identical domains; for instance, example.com might become exanple.com. Attackers can register thousands of domains differing from target organizations' URLs by a single character for reasons ranging from suspicious to fully malicious. Rogue websites using these modified domain names are built to look like legitimate websites. The rogue domains and websites can be used in spearphishing campaigns against company employees or customers, watering-hole attacks, and drive-by download attacks.

Being alerted to newly registered phishing and typosquatting domains in real time narrows the window available for cybercriminals to impersonate your brand to defraud unsuspecting users. Once this malicious infrastructure is identified, you can employ a takedown service to nullify the threat.

ON THE WEB

We've already seen that criminal forums and marketplaces are well known for facilitating all types of clandestine transactions. But these channels are not the exclusive domain of criminal outsiders. A report from Recorded Future describes how corporate insiders advertise their access to criminal actors, as well as how employees and contractors are recruited into the criminal underground. Insiders are a useful cog in the machinery of fraud, from retail cash-out services, to carding operations, to theft facilitation by bank employees. Read the report "Insider Threats to Financial Services: Uncovering Evidence With External Intelligence."

Chapter 8

Analytical Frameworks for Threat Intelligence

- Learn about the advantages of using threat intelligence frameworks
- Understand the strengths and weaknesses of the three best-known frameworks
- See how the three frameworks can complement each other

"Structure is required for creativity."

— Twyla Tharp

Threat intelligence frameworks provide structures for thinking about attacks and adversaries. They promote a broad understanding of how attackers think, the methods they use, and where in an attack lifecycle specific events occur. This knowledge allows defenders to take decisive action faster and stop attackers sooner.

Frameworks also help focus attention on details that require further investigation to ensure that threats have been fully removed, and that measures are put in place to prevent future intrusions of the same kind.

Finally, frameworks are useful for sharing information within and across organizations. They provide a common grammar and syntax for explaining the details of attacks and how those details relate to each other. A shared framework makes it easier to ingest threat intelligence from sources such as threat intelligence vendors, open source forums, and information sharing and analysis centers (ISACs).

TIP

The frameworks outlined below are not competitive, but rather complementary. You can utilize one, two, or all three of them.

The Lockheed Martin Cyber Kill Chain®

The Cyber Kill Chain®, first developed by Lockheed Martin in 2011, is the best known of the cyber threat intelligence frameworks. The Cyber Kill Chain is based on the military concept of the kill chain, which breaks the structure of an attack into stages. By breaking an attack up in this manner, defenders can pinpoint which stage it is in and deploy appropriate countermeasures.

The Cyber Kill Chain describes seven stages of an attack:

1. Reconnaissance
2. Weaponization
3. Delivery
4. Exploitation
5. Installation
6. Command and Control
7. Actions and Objectives (sometimes referred to as exfiltration)

These stages are often laid out in a diagram similar to Figure 8-1.

Figure 8-1: Diagram of the Lockheed Martin Cyber Kill Chain.

Security teams can develop standard responses for each stage.

For example, if you manage to stop an attack at the exploitation stage, you can have high confidence that nothing has been installed on the targeted systems and full incident response activity may not be needed.

The Cyber Kill Chain also allows organizations to build a defense-in-depth model that targets specific parts of the kill chain. For example, you might acquire third-party threat intelligence specifically to monitor:

- ☑ References to your enterprise on the web that would indicate reconnaissance activities
- ☑ Information about weaponization against newly reported vulnerabilities in applications on your network

Limitations of the Cyber Kill Chain

The Cyber Kill Chain is a good way to start thinking about how to defend against attacks, but it has some limitations. One of the big criticisms of this model is that it doesn't take into account the way many modern attacks work. For example, many phishing attacks skip the exploitation phase entirely, and instead rely on the victim to open a Microsoft Office document with an embedded macro or to double-click on an attached script.

But even with these limitations, the Cyber Kill Chain creates a good baseline to discuss attacks and where they can be stopped. It also makes it easier to share information about attacks within and outside of the organization using standard, well-defined attack points.

 ON THE WEB You can find out more about the Cyber Kill Chain by reading the seminal white paper and visiting the Cyber Kill Chain website.

The Diamond Model

The Diamond Model was created in 2013 by researchers at the now-defunct Center for Cyber Intelligence Analysis and Threat Research (CCIATR). It is used to track attack groups over time rather than the progress of individual attacks.

In its simplest form, the Diamond Model looks similar to Figure 8-2. It is used to classify the different elements of an attack. The diamond for an attacker or attack group is not static, but rather evolves as the attacker changes infrastructure and targets and modifies TTPs.

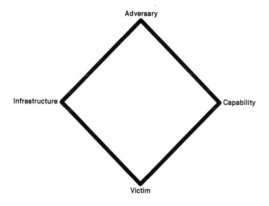

Figure 8-2: A simple Diamond Model design.

The Diamond Model helps defenders track an attacker, the victims, the attacker's capabilities, and the infrastructure the attacker uses. Each of the points on the diamond is a pivot point that defenders can use during an investigation to connect one aspect of an attack with the others.

Pivoting

Let's say you uncover command and control traffic to a suspicious IP address. The Diamond Model would help you "pivot" from this initial indicator to find information about the attacker associated with that IP address, then research the known capabilities of that attacker. Knowing those capabilities will enable you to respond more quickly and effectively to the incident. Or imagine that your threat intelligence solution uses the Diamond Model. If the board of directors asks who is launching similar attacks against other organizations in your industry (attribution), you may be able to quickly find a list of victims, the probable attacker, and a description of that attacker's TTPs. These will help you decide what defenses need to be put in place.

Flexibility

One of the big advantages of the Diamond Model is its flexibility and extensibility. You can add different aspects of an attack under the appropriate point on the diamond to create complex profiles of different attack groups. Other features of an attack that can be tracked include:

1. Phase
2. Result
3. Direction
4. Methodology
5. Resources

Challenges with the Diamond Model

The downside is that Diamond Models require a lot of care and feeding. Some aspects of the model, especially infrastructure, change rapidly. If you don't update the diamond of an attacker constantly, you run the risk of working with outdated information.

TIP

Time stamp every update of a diamond so everybody has visibility into the age of the information.

TIP

If you don't have the time and resources to manage this type of model yourself, you may be able to get updated information from a third-party threat intelligence provider.

Even with these challenges, though, the Diamond Model can make the jobs of many security people easier by helping get everyone fast answers about threats.

ON THE WEB

To learn more about the Diamond Model, read the Recorded Future blog post "Applying Threat Intelligence to the Diamond Model of Intrusion Analysis", or download the original white paper "The Diamond Model of Intrusion Analysis."

The MITRE ATT&CK™ Framework

MITRE is a unique organization in the United States: a corporation responsible for managing federal funding for research projects across multiple federal agencies. It has had a huge impact on the security industry, including the development and maintenance of the Common Vulnerabilities and Exposures (CVE) and the Common Weakness Enumeration (CWE) databases.

MITRE has developed a number of other frameworks that are very important for threat intelligence, including:

- ☑ The Trusted Automated Exchange of Intelligence Information (TAXII™), a transport protocol that enables organizations to share threat intelligence over HTTPS and use common application programming interface (API) commands to extract that threat intelligence
- ☑ Structured Threat Information eXpression (STIX™), a standardized format for presenting threat intelligence information
- ☑ The Cyber Observable eXpression (CybOX™) framework, a method for tracking observables from cybersecurity incidents

Categories of attacker behavior

The MITRE Adversarial Tactics, Techniques, and Common Knowledge (ATT&CK™) framework was created as a means of tracking adversarial behavior over time. ATT&CK builds on the Cyber Kill Chain, but rather than describe a single attack, it focuses on the indicators and tactics associated with specific adversaries.

ATT&CK uses 11 different tactic categories to describe adversary behavior:

1. Initial Access
2. Execution
3. Persistence
4. Privilege Escalation
5. Defense Evasion
6. Credential Access
7. Discovery

8. Lateral Movement

9. Collection

10. Exfiltration

11. Command and Control

Each of these tactical categories includes individual techniques that can be used to describe the adversary's behavior. For example, under the Initial Access category, behaviors include Spearphishing Attachment, Spearphishing Link, Trusted Relationship, and Valid Accounts.

 ON THE WEB You can see the MITRE Enterprise ATT&CK Framework at https://attack.mitre.org/wiki/Main_Page.

This classification of behaviors allows security teams to be very granular in describing and tracking adversarial behavior and makes it easy to share information between teams.

ATT&CK™ is useful across a wide range of security functions, from threat intelligence analysts to SOC operators and incident response teams. Tracking adversary behavior in a structured and repeatable way allows teams to:

- ☑ Prioritize incident response

- ☑ Tie indicators to attackers

- ☑ Identify holes in an organization's security posture

 TIP Threat intelligence frameworks help codify the way your security teams look at threats, indicators, vulnerabilities, and actors. If you are not prepared to build out your own framework for analysis, consider partnering with security companies that have solutions built around these frameworks. That approach enables you to enjoy the benefits of the framework quickly and makes your security activities much more effective.

Chapter 9

Your Threat Intelligence Journey

In this chapter

- Review ways to clarify your threat intelligence needs and goals
- Examine key success factors that contribute to effective programs
- Learn how to start simple and scale up

"Whatever you do, or dream you can, begin it. Boldness has genius and power and magic in it."

— Johann Wolfgang von Goethe

In this chapter of our book, we suggest some do's and don'ts for starting on your threat intelligence journey and steering toward a comprehensive program.

Don't Start With Threat Feeds

In the first chapter we discussed several common misconceptions about threat intelligence, including that it is mostly about threat data feeds. In fact, many organizations begin their threat intelligence programs by signing up for threat data feeds and connecting them with a SIEM solution.

This may seem like a good way to start because many threat data feeds are open source (i.e., free), and the technical indicators they deliver appear useful and easy to interpret. Since all malware is bad, and every suspicious URL could be used by an attacker, the more clues you have about them the better, right?

Well, in reality, the vast majority of malware samples and suspicious URLs are not related to current threats to your enterprise. That's why feeding large volumes of unfiltered threat data to your SIEM will almost certainly create the kind of alert fatigue we examined in Chapter 3.

ON THE WEB To learn more about the range of threat intelligence sources, take a look at the Recorded Future blog post "Beyond Feeds: A Deep Dive Into Threat Intelligence Sources."

Clarify Your Threat Intelligence Needs and Goals

Because threat intelligence provides value to so many teams in cybersecurity, it is important to develop priorities that reflect the overall needs and goals of the enterprise.

Answer these questions

Rather than assuming that any one team, data source, or threat intelligence technology should have priority, you should develop a clear set of goals by determining the needs of each security group in your organization and the advantages that threat intelligence can bring to them.

Begin by considering these questions:

- ☑ What are your greatest risks?
- ☑ What are the ways that threat intelligence can help address each of those risks?
- ☑ What is the potential impact of addressing each risk?
- ☑ What gaps need to be filled by information, technology, or human resources to make threat intelligence effective in those areas?

Answering these questions will help you clarify where threat intelligence can deliver the biggest gains in the shortest time. It will also guide your investigation of which threat intelligence sources, tools, and vendors can best support you and what staff you need to strengthen your program.

ON THE WEB The Recorded Future white paper "Best Practices for Applying Threat Intelligence" elaborates on why it is better to start out not by investigating technologies or vendors, but by looking first at the types of threat intelligence that are available and how they can make different areas of cybersecurity more effective.

Identify teams that can benefit most from threat intelligence

Teams across your security organization can benefit from intelligence that drives informed decision making and offers unique perspectives. Intelligence that is comprehensive, relevant, and easy to consume has the potential to revolutionize how different roles in your organization operate day to day. Figure 9-1 shows examples of how teams inside organizations can use threat intelligence.

Figure 9-1: How security teams use threat intelligence.

When determining how to move your threat intelligence strategy forward, it's important to identify all the potential users in your organization and align the intelligence to their unique use cases.

DON'T FORGET Drill down into the types of threat intelligence each group can use and exactly how they will benefit in terms of faster responses, lower costs, better use of staff, better investment decisions, etc. Often the needs and benefits are not obvious. Documenting these details will help you set priorities, justify investments, and find surprising new uses for threat intelligence.

ON THE WEB Learn how threat intelligence can compensate for the talent gap that many companies face by reading the Recorded Future blog post "Threat Analyst Insights: Threat Intelligence as a Leveler."

Key Success Factors

We have observed several factors that frequently contribute to effective threat intelligence programs.

Generating quick wins with monitoring

Monitoring threat information can provide quick benefits with relatively modest investments. The key is to look for a few types of data that are particularly meaningful for your business and information security strategy and will help you anticipate emerging threats or provide early warning of actual attacks. Your activities might include things like:

- ☑ Checking for new vulnerabilities that affect your most important software packages, servers, and endpoints
- ☑ Tracking threat trends that pose potential risks to your business operations
- ☑ Watching for any leaked corporate credentials, data, or code appearing on public or dark web sites

There are probably a few data types that are vitally important to your business and that you can monitor without investing in new infrastructure or staff. Monitoring them can generate quick wins, demonstrate the advantages of threat intelligence, and build enthusiasm for the program.

Automating as much as possible

Effective threat intelligence programs typically focus on automation from the beginning. They start by automating fundamental tasks like data aggregation, comparison, labeling, and contextualization. When these tasks are performed by machines, humans are freed up to work on making effective, informed decisions.

As your threat intelligence program becomes more sophisticated, you may find even more opportunities for automation. You will be able to automate information sharing among a larger group of security solutions and automate more workflows that provide intelligence to incident analysis and response and fraud prevention teams. You will be able to offload more of the "thinking" to your threat intelligence solutions, for example, by having the software automatically correlate threat data and produce risk scores.

CAUTION

When you evaluate threat intelligence solutions, examine the level to which they employ automation. Is automation confined to aggregating and cross-referencing data, or does the solution add context that equips your teams to make risk-based decisions with confidence? Keep in mind that in threat intelligence, more raw data only adds value if it's properly analyzed, structured, and delivered to you in an easy-to-consume format.

Integrating threat intelligence with processes and infrastructure

Integrating threat intelligence tools with existing systems is an effective way to make the intelligence accessible and usable without overwhelming teams with new technologies.

Part of integration is giving threat intelligence tools visibility into the security events and activities captured by your other security and network tools. Combining and correlating internal and external data points can produce genuine intelligence that is both relevant to your business and placed in the context of the wider threat landscape.

The other critical aspect of integration is delivering the most important, specific, relevant, and contextualized intelligence to the right group at the right time.

Threat intelligence solutions can be integrated with SIEMs and other security tools either through APIs or interfaces developed in partnership with the security tool vendors.

TIP

When you evaluate threat intelligence solutions, it's important to understand which ones can integrate with your existing software and support your security teams' use cases.

Getting expert help to nurture internal experts

The value you get from threat intelligence is directly related to your ability to make it relevant to your organization and apply it to existing and new security processes.

You can reach these goals faster if you work with a vendor or consultant that provides both technical capabilities and expertise to empower your organization to get the most from threat intelligence. As time goes on, working with such a partner will enable members of your team to become threat intelligence experts in their own right, so that your capabilities in the field can grow organically.

DON'T FORGET

Look for partners with a wide and deep bench of threat intelligence experts. These specialists should be equipped to understand your needs and ready to help you get the most from your investment. You should be able to call on their expertise as needed and to work with them to identify new advantages from leveraging threat intelligence in your organization. Your chosen partners should not only help you succeed today, but also support your security teams as you move forward.

ON THE WEB

You can get more information on selecting the right threat intelligence solution by downloading "The Buyer's Guide to Cyber Threat Intelligence," from Recorded Future. It includes a handy RFP template to use in evaluating the capabilities of different vendors.

Start Simple and Scale Up

We hope this book has shown you that threat intelligence is not some kind of monolith that needs to be dropped onto the security organization all at one time. Instead, you have options to draw on a wide range of data sources and then process, analyze, and disseminate threat intelligence to every major group in cybersecurity.

That means you can start simple with your current staff (instead of a dedicated threat intelligence group), a few data sources, and integration with existing security tools like SIEM and vulnerability management systems. You can then scale up to dedicated staffing, more data sources, more tools, more integration, and more automated workflows, as shown in Figure 9-2.

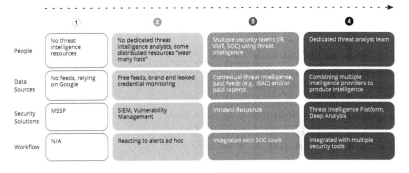

Figure 9-2: Four stages of maturity for threat intelligence programs, from no internal resources, to limited sources and tools, to a fully staffed, highly automated threat intelligence program.

Start the journey by researching the needs of each group in your cybersecurity organization and seeing how threat intelligence can help them achieve their objectives.

Then, over time, you can build toward a comprehensive threat intelligence program that:

- ☑ Scours the widest possible range of technical, open, and dark web sources
- ☑ Uses automation to deliver easily consumable intelligence
- ☑ Provides fully contextualized alerts in real time with limited false positives
- ☑ Integrates with and enhances existing security technologies and processes
- ☑ Consistently improves the efficiency and efficacy of your entire security organization

Chapter 10

Developing the Core Threat Intelligence Team

In this chapter

- Understand the processes, people, and technology that make up a dedicated threat intelligence capability
- Learn how these teams use threat intelligence not just to judge risk, but also to drive business continuity
- Review ways to engage with threat intelligence communities

"Talent wins games, but teamwork and intelligence win championships."

— Michael Jordan

We have seen how threat intelligence benefits most of the teams in the information security organization. We now make a few suggestions about how to organize your core threat intelligence team itself.

Dedicated, but Not Necessarily Separate

As we discussed in the previous chapter, you can start your threat intelligence journey with people who continue to play other roles on different teams in the organization.

Two questions will arise:

1. Should there be a dedicated threat intelligence team?
2. Should it be independent, or can it live inside another cybersecurity group?

The answers are: yes, and it depends.

A dedicated team is best

As you develop a comprehensive threat intelligence program, you should build a team dedicated to collecting and analyzing threat data and turning it into intelligence. The sole focus of this team should be to provide relevant and actionable intelligence to key stakeholders, including senior executives and members of the board.

Dedication and a broad perspective are needed to ensure team members dedicate enough time to collecting, processing, analyzing, and disseminating intelligence that provides the greatest value to the enterprise as a whole, rather than yielding to the temptation to focus on the intelligence needs of one group or another.

Its location depends on your organization

Organizational independence, as shown in Figure 10-1, has its advantages, such as greater autonomy and prestige.

Figure 10-1: Threat intelligence as an independent group in the cybersecurity organizational structure.

However, these advantages can be completely offset by the jealousies and political issues caused by creating a team with a new high-level manager and its own budget that pulls budding threat intelligence analysts out of their existing groups.

A dedicated threat intelligence team does not necessarily need to be a separate function reporting directly to a VP or the CISO. It can belong to a group that already works with threat intelligence. In many cases this will be the incident response group. This savvy approach can avoid conflict with entrenched security teams.

Picking the People

If you take a gradual approach to building your core threat intelligence team, start with individuals who are already in the cybersecurity organization and are applying threat intelligence to their particular areas of security. They may not have the title "threat intelligence analyst" or see themselves that way at first, but they can form the backbone of your emerging threat intelligence capability.

For an example of how one security analyst transitioned to a full-time threat intelligence role, read the Recorded Future blog post "Changing Hats: From Enterprise Security to Threat Intelligence as a Service."

Core Competencies

We have emphasized that the threat intelligence function exists to strengthen other teams in the cybersecurity organization so they can better protect a specific enterprise. It is therefore critical that the threat intelligence team include people who understand the core business, operational workflows, network infrastructure, risk profiles, and supply chain as well as the technical infrastructure and software applications of the entire enterprise.

As the threat intelligence team matures, you'll want to add members with skills for:

☑ Correlating external data with internal telemetry

☑ Providing threat situational awareness and recommendations for security controls

☑ Proactively hunting internal threats, including insider threats

☑ Educating employees and customers on cyber threats

☑ Engaging with the wider threat intelligence community

☑ Identifying and managing information sources

The Four Types of Threat Intelligence

A threat intelligence team needs to plan and allocate resources to address the four types of threat intelligence shown in Figure 10-2.

Figure 10-2: Types of threat intelligence. (Source NCSC UK, MWR)

Strategic threat intelligence provides a wide view of the threat environment and business issues. It is designed to inform the decisions of executive boards and senior officers. Strategic threat intelligence usually is not overtly technical, and is most likely to cover topics such as the financial impact of cybersecurity or major regulatory changes.

Tactical threat intelligence focuses on attackers' tactics, techniques, and procedures (TTPs). It relates to the specific attack vectors favored by threat actors in your industry or geographic location. Typically this form of intelligence is highly actionable and is used by operational staff such as incident responders to ensure technical controls and processes are suitably prepared.

Operational threat intelligence is related to specific, impending attacks. It helps senior security staff anticipate when and where attacks will come.

Technical threat intelligence comprises a stream of indicators that can be used to automatically identify and block suspected malicious communications.

Scenarios for Using the Four Types of Threat Intelligence

If your business is looking to move towards integrating with an AI assistant like Amazon Alexa or allowing customers to transact with Bitcoin, **strategic threat intelligence** can highlight the risk factors in these initiatives and make suggestions for mitigation.

If spearphishing is identified as a prominent attack vector in your industry, **tactical threat intelligence** could show how additional security training for highly privileged users can foil those attacks.

If you want to identify individuals planning to attack your business or customers, **operational threat intelligence** might provide answers by monitoring information from criminal communities on the dark web.

If you want to prevent stolen data from being exfiltrated from your network, **technical threat intelligence** might highlight an IP address suspected to be malicious, allowing you to block communication with that address. Technical threat intelligence is typically transient and available in extremely high volumes, so you should find ways to process it automatically rather than involving human analysts.

Collecting and Enriching Threat Data

We talked a little about sources of threat data in Chapter 1. Here we explore how a threat intelligence team can work with a range of sources to ensure accuracy and relevance.

The human edge

Threat intelligence vendors can provide some types of strategic intelligence, but you can also develop in-house capabilities to gather information about the topics and events most relevant to your enterprise.

For example, you could develop an internal web crawler that analyzes the web page code of the top 5,000 web destinations visited by your employees. This analysis might provide insights into the potential for drive-by download attacks. You could share the insights with the security architecture team to help them propose controls that defend against those attacks. This kind of threat intelligence generates concrete data, which is much more useful than anecdotes, conjecture, and generic statistics about attacks.

Additional sources

Proprietary sources that can strengthen your threat intelligence resources include:

- ☑ Vendor or ISAC feeds
- ☑ Whitelists
- ☑ Blacklists
- ☑ Threat intelligence team research

Combining sources

An automated threat intelligence solution enables the threat intelligence team to centralize, combine, and enrich data from multiple sources before the data is ingested by other security systems or viewed by human analysts on security operations teams.

Figure 10-3 shows the elements of such an automated threat solution. In this process, information from a threat intelligence vendor is filtered to find data that is important to the enterprise and specific cybersecurity teams. Then it is enriched by data from internal threat intelligence sources and output in formats appropriate for targets such as SIEMs and incident response systems. This automated translation of data into relevant insights is the very essence of threat intelligence.

Figure 10-3: A threat intelligence platform can centralize, combine, and enrich data, then format it for multiple target systems. (Source: Recorded Future)

The role of intelligent machines

Advances in machine learning and natural language processing (NLP) can bring additional advantages to the threat intelligence team. With the right technology, references to threats from all sources can be rendered language-neutral, so it can be analyzed by humans and machines regardless of the original language used. We've reached the point where AI components have successfully learned the language of threats and can accurately identify "malicious" terms.

The combination of machine learning, NLP, and AI offers huge opportunities for organizations to leverage threat intelligence. Not only can these technologies remove language barriers, but they also can reduce analyst workloads by taking on many tasks related to data collection and correlation. When combined with the power to consider multiple data and information sources concurrently to produce genuine threat intelligence, these capabilities make it far easier to build a comprehensible map of the threat landscape.

ON THE WEB See how Recorded Future applies advanced AI in the white paper "4 Ways Machine Learning Is Powering Smarter Threat Intelligence."

ON THE WEB You can find out how financial services giant Fannie Mae streamlined the communication of finished intelligence by reading "How to Build a Cyber Threat Intelligence Team (and Why Technology Isn't Enough)" on the Recorded Future blog.

Engaging With Threat Intelligence Communities

Threat intelligence cannot flourish in a vacuum. External relationships are the lifeblood of successful threat intelligence teams. No matter how advanced your team might be, no single group can be as smart individually as the threat intelligence world as a whole.

Many threat intelligence communities allow individual enterprises to share relevant and timely attack data so they can protect themselves before they are victimized. Engaging with trusted communities such as ISACs is crucial for decreasing risk, not just for your individual enterprises, but also for the entire industry and the cybersecurity world at large. Participation requires time and resources, for example to communicate with peers via email and to attend security conferences, but relationship building must be a priority for threat intelligence to be successful.

Conclusion

"Know your enemy and know yourself and you can fight a hundred battles without disaster."

– Sun Tzu

Two Key Takeaways From the Book

We began this guide by introducing the premise that intelligence helps everyone in cybersecurity, enabling teams to anticipate threats, respond to attacks faster, and make better decisions on how to reduce risk. In the 10 chapters contained in this book, we examined how intelligence can be applied to numerous facets of an organization's security strategy.

Although the applications for intelligence vary significantly, from strategic to highly technical, there are two key themes that apply to all. Firstly, intelligence provides critical insight into the real risks your organization faces. Secondly, true intelligence can streamline how teams work to make better use of valuable human resources.

A focus on relevant risk

It is accepted wisdom that there is no such thing as being "one hundred percent secure." This highlights the importance of relevance when it comes to identifying and responding to threats. The more confident you can be that the intelligence in your hands is directly relevant to the security of your enterprise, the more effective you will be at actually reducing the risk those threats present.

Increased efficiency makes for better security

Making the best use of the highly skilled individuals that comprise your security teams is also critical for mounting an effective defense. Integrated threat intelligence is proven to help security teams identify threats earlier and resolve incidents faster.

Whether you are just kicking off your threat intelligence initiative or you are many years into your strategy, efficiently reducing risk is the ultimate goal.

Appendix
Threat Intelligence Goals: A Quick Reference Guide

Threat intelligence is not "one size fits all." The security applications of threat intelligence in your business depend on the nature of your organization and your existing information security strategies and capabilities.

This library of threat intelligence goals aligns with the security teams we have highlighted in this book. You can use these goals to help identify and prioritize threat intelligence activities.

Security Operations	
Data Exposure Incidents	Report data exposure incidents to affected stakeholders for remediation
High-Risk Malware Families	Research evolution and trends of malware families with high risk to my organization
Reputation Risk	Identify risks to my organization's reputation
Incident Response	
Data Exposure Incidents	Report data exposure incidents to affected parties and stakeholders for remediation
Vulnerability Management	
Exploit Kits	Identify information about exploit kits
High-Risk Vulnerabilites	Identify critical and high-risk vulnerabilities in tech stack
Undisclosed Vulnerabilities	Identify undisclosed zero-day and embargoed vulnerabilities
Risk Analysis	
Third-Party Security Competence	Assess third party's information security competence
Third Parties With Elevated Risk	Identify third parties that have elevated risk to my organization
Competitive Research	Research competitive market
Security Leadership	
Third Parties With Elevated Risk	Identify third parties that have elevated risk to my organization
Attack Planning	Identify attack planning that could target my organization

Industry Attack Trends	Identify campaigns targeting related industries
Infrastructure Risk	Increased risk score for my infrastructure
Phishing and Spam Campaign Trends	Identify trending campaigns that use spearphishing or phishing with malicious email attachments or links
Reputation Risk	Identify risks to my organization's reputation
Targeted Campaign Research	Identify IOCs associated with a specific operation or campaign to help track and mitigate cyberattacks
Targeted Threat Actor Research	Identify IOCs associated with threat actors to help track and mitigate cyberattacks
Fraud Prevention	
Stolen Asset Discovery	Discover stolen assets (e.g., gift cards, credit cards) posted online
Threat Intelligence Analysis	
Third Parties With Elevated Risk	Identify third parties that have elevated risk to my organization
Data Exposure Incidents	Report data exposure incidents to affected parties and stakeholders for remediation
Exploit Kits	Identify information about exploit kits
High-Risk Malware Families	Research evolution and trends of malware families with high risk to me
High-Risk Vulnerabilities	Identify critical and high-risk vulnerabilities in tech stack
Identify Attack Planning	Identify attack planning that could target my organization
Industry Attack Trends	Identify campaigns targeting related industries
Infrastructure Risk	Increased risk score for my infrastructure
Phishing and Spam Campaign Trends	Identify trending campaigns that use spearphishing or phishing with malicious email attachments or links
Reputation Risk	Identify risks to my organization's reputation
Targeted Campaign Research	Identify IOCs associated with a specific operation or campaign to help track and mitigate cyberattacks
Targeted Threat Actor Research	Identify IOCs associated with threat actors to help track and mitigate cyberattacks
Undisclosed Vulnerabilities	Identify undisclosed zero-day and embargoed vulnerabilities